Midnight on Mourn Street

A Play in Two Acts

Christopher Conlon

Midnight on Mourn Street
A Play in Two Acts

by Christopher Conlon
©2010 Christopher Conlon

Published in Canada
Creative Guy Publishing
Vancouver BC
First Printing June 2010
ISBN 9781894953696

Cover photo, "Couple at Foggy Night."
©2010 Piotr Rydzkowski and used under license.

Library and Archives Canada Cataloguing in Publication

Conlon, Christopher, 1962-
Midnight on Mourn Street : a play in two
acts / Christopher Conlon.

Adapted from the author's novel of the same name.
Also issued in electronic format.
ISBN 978-1-894953-69-6

I. Title.

PS3603.O5585M53 2010 812'.6 C2010-902878-3

Acclaim for *Midnight on Mourn Street*

"As an admirer of the original novel of *Midnight on Mourn Street*, I was wondering how Christopher Conlon would manage to convey the story's intricate and intimate twists and emotions within the confines of a theater stage…and, if anything, he's managed to distill the tale down into something even more poignant, shocking, and tragic. *Midnight on Mourn Street* works so well as a play that it makes me wish I magically had access to a 400-seat house, three of the best actors in the world, and the skills to direct it…but in the meantime, it plays beautifully in the theater of the mind. Conlon has crafted both a superb example of the difficult art of adaptation, and an enthralling and deeply moving stand-alone read."
—Three-time Bram Stoker Award-winner **Lisa Morton**, author of *The Castle of Los Angeles*

"With his stage adaptation of *Midnight on Mourn Street*, Christopher Conlon has pulled an amazing emotional sleight-of-hand: he has brilliantly translated an intensely introverted novel into a celebration of the spoken word and in-depth characterization. One should read both the novel and the stage adaptation back-to-back for a perfect lesson on how transferring one form of storytelling media into another can produce new insight to the core work. This is quite simply, in my eyes, an amazing achievement."
—Five-time Bram Stoker Award-winner **Gary A. Braunbeck**, author of *A Cracked and Broken Path*

Midnight on Mourn Street

A Play in Two Acts

Christopher Conlon

creative guy publishing
vancouver | canada

Table of Contents

The Characters

Reed Waters—tall, thin, about 40. Caucasian. He dresses in a nondescript fashion—plain work shirts, trousers or jeans, tennis shoes or loafers. A man who tries hard to go unnoticed.

Mauri Dyson—about 15. Caucasian. Old jeans, flashy abbreviated tops, tattered tennis shoes. Her hair should have an outrageous quality— bizarre artificial coloring or spikes, perhaps. But it should look cheap and homemade, not as if she's come from a fashion salon.

Will Bliss—17 or 18, a handsome African-American boy from a rough neighborhood who doesn't, at least externally, show it. Will dresses very nattily—collegiate pullover sweaters, slacks, loafers. He wears glasses.

The Set

The living room of one-bedroom apartment. A somewhat tattered sofa is the dominant feature. The sofa faces an unseen "fireplace" downstage; a few fireplace tools in a rack are nearby. One or two chairs around the living room area. A bookshelf or two, stuffed with books, CDs, and a small stereo unit. Farther upstage, to one side, is a small breakfast table with chairs. A tiny television is near it, possibly on the table itself. At the rear of the stage is the kitchen of the apartment, with stove and oven, refrigerator, microwave, etc. An exit upstage to one side serves as the entrance to the apartment's single bedroom and bathroom. To one side there is a door leading out. Next to it is a window (suggested by a supported window frame).

On each side of the apartment is a small playing area in which the characters appear outside.

MIDNIGHT ON MOURN STREET

Act 1

Scene One

Sound of rain.

Offstage, Reed cries out.

Lights up—dimly, suggesting night—as, a moment later, phone rings. Reed appears from back bedroom to answer. He is dressed but disheveled, shaking his head, having just awakened.

Outside, Mauri appears, inadequately dressed for the weather, obviously cold and wet, coughing. She carries a small battered backpack. She looks at the building before her.

REED: *(switches on lamp, picks up phone)* Yes?... Oh, Will, how are you?... Well, if I sound sleepy, it's because I've been sleeping... I know, I know, it's early... I just laid down for a moment and fell asleep... I'm an old man, my friend. Give me a break. I just had the most terrible nightmare... My head is still fuzzy.

> *Mauri wanders around building front, touching wall, trying to peer in through window, during dialogue.*

REED: Yes, sure. Tomorrow's Saturday. I'll take you to the university library. What's the topic of your paper again—Richard Wright? Sure. We'll find loads of things...I know, but you're a senior now, Will. It's time to stop relying on the Internet. You need to use actual books from time to time....That's right. Those small objects with the paper sheets in them. *(Chuckles)* What's that? Well, hum it to me...*(Listens)* Oh, yes...Do you mean this?

3

He hums the famous melody from the first movement of Tchaikovsky's 1st Piano Concerto.

That's Tchaikovsky. His first piano concerto… Right, the 1812 Overture guy, that's him…No, no need to buy it. I have it here. You can borrow it tomorrow. Okay…? Good. Well, I'll see you, then. How's your mother…? And all those siblings of yours…? *(Long pause; chuckles)* Really? My goodness. Well, yes. Okay. Tomorrow. You'll come by here? And we'll go? Great. Bye-bye, Will.

He hangs up, switches on another light or two, goes toward kitchen humming. Pours coffee from pot on stove into cup, stands drinking. At the same time Mauri sits heavily under the window outside. She begins to cry, not showily, but with enough volume that Reed hears her. She removes what is clearly a bottle of alcohol from her backpack and takes a large swig. Reed looks curiously about, finally gazing through window, puzzled. He sees nothing. He goes to table with his cup, sits, looks absently through a newspaper or magazine for a few moments. The crying is distracting to him. He gets up, looks out again, finally goes to front door and opens it. Glances up at the rain, holds his hand over his eyes as a visor. He sees her, approaches.

REED: Excuse me?

Mauri's head shoots up, surprised. She stops crying, stands quickly.

REED: Are you all right?

She backs away from him, suspicious.

REED: I mean—it looks like you're camping out on my lawn…It's not a good night for it. You'll get soaked.

4

MAURI: I'm okay.

REED: What?

MAURI: I said I'm okay. *(Coughs)*

REED: You don't—well, you don't look okay. Do you need an umbrella?

MAURI: No. I'm fine.

REED: Well—are you staying out here?

MAURI: No. I'll go. I'm sorry to bother you, mister.

> *She turns to leave, makes it a few steps, then something seems to overwhelm her. Her knees buckle. She sways. Reed rushes to her.*

REED: You're *not* okay.

> *She falls into his arms, shaking.*

REED: What's wrong? What is it?

> *But she seems unable to respond, makes only indistinct sounds. He looks up at the rain, wipes his eyes.*

REED: You can't stay out here. Come on, come in.

> *He helps her toward the door. Her head sways; she is semi-conscious. When they arrive at the door she protests weakly.*

MAURI: What...? No, no....

REED: It's all right. Just come in where it's dry and you can sit down.

MAURI: I—can't...

REED: Just for a few minutes. Until you feel stronger. Please. Look, my name's Reed. What's yours?

MAURI: My...?

REED: Your name. What's your name?

MAURI: *(Indistinct sounds)*

REED: Never mind. Just come in.

> *As she crosses the threshold of the door she suddenly cries out, draws back.*

REED: It's all right. Really. Don't be afraid. No one should be left out in the rain.

> *She allows herself to be led in. He directs her to the sofa, where she immediately drops down—virtually collapses.*

MAURI: I'll be okay in a minute—I'm just dizzy...

REED: Are you hungry? I could call the hospital—I could drive you there if you want—it's not far...

MAURI: I just need my head to settle for a minute. It's spinning...

REED: Have you eaten lately?

MAURI: Stole some Slim Jims from a 7-Eleven...That was this morning.

REED: That's all?

MAURI: I think so...

> *Reed goes to kitchen, begins quickly assembling food on a plate. He pours her a glass of milk from the refrigerator.*

6

REED: That's not good, you know. That's not good at all. Not eating will make you sick, it... *(Nervous, keeping a flow of chatter as he puts together the food)* Especially for a young girl like you, you really need...You shouldn't allow yourself to go hungry like that. It's...it's very...I don't have a lot here, if I'd realized I was going to have company I would have brought in some things...I don't eat a lot myself, and what I do eat is pretty simple fare...So I can't offer a lot of...Well...Anyway, here are some things. Let's just see, okay? Let's see if some food helps. *(He brings the plate and glass to her.)* Can you sit up?

> *She does. She looks at the plate and glass for a moment, then takes them hastily and begins wolfing everything down. Reed watches her for a moment, then turns self-consciously away and crouches before the "fireplace," takes out a match and lights it, takes a fireplace tool and gives the fire a poke or two.*

REED: These artificial logs are—are great. They light just like that. Their flames are just slow and steady, no popping, no sparks. And hardly any ash afterward. I always keep one in here, around this time. Fall, winter... *(Pause, stepping back to look at the fire, glancing at her)* It's not every day I bring in a camper from my front lawn, you know. I—I don't often have company.

> *She is preoccupied with the food; doesn't respond.*

REED: I—I didn't get your name....

> *Still no response. Finally he moves to the window.*

REED: The rain isn't letting up, is it? Terrible night. It's going to rain for hours, the weatherman said. It's supposed to let up toward dawn. November is too early in the season for snow—at least you missed that. But—but the rain is cold, it's very cold...

> *At last she finishes, puts the plate and glass aside, wipes her mouth on her sleeve, perhaps burps.*

7

REED: Have you had enough to eat?

She looks at him.

REED: You look like you're feeling a little better.

MAURI: The fire's nice. *(Turns to it)*

REED: Good.

MAURI: I can't believe I, like, fainted. I thought that was just something people did in old movies.

REED: I was afraid I was going to have to call 911.

MAURI: Sorry.

REED: You haven't told me your name.

MAURI: It's Mauri. Mauri Stevens.

REED: Well, Mauri Stevens, I'm Reed Waters. Pleased to meet you.

MAURI: I'll be out of here in just a couple of minutes, Mr. Waters.

REED: Reed. And you don't have to hurry. It's bad out there. Listen to that rain.

MAURI: I'll be okay. Don't worry about me.

REED: Do you live around here?

MAURI: No. I don't live around here. I've never been in D.C. before.

REED: What…Well, what brings you to our nation's capital?

She shrugs.

REED: I didn't mean to pry. I'm sorry.

8

MAURI: No, it doesn't matter. I'm here to find someone.

REED: A friend?

MAURI: No. Not a friend.

REED: Oh. Have you been here long? In the city?

MAURI: Just got here today.

REED: Where from? If you don't mind my asking.

She stretches out her shoes toward the fire.

MAURI: Mind if I take my shoes off?

REED: Of course not. Go ahead. *(She does.)*

MAURI: My socks are wet, too.

REED: I've got a clothes dryer…

MAURI: No, it's okay. I'll just put them in front of the fire here. *(She takes off her socks, places them before her, stretches her feet toward the flames.)* Oh, that's nice. That's *good.*

Reed gets up, goes to kitchen to refill his cup. He doesn't notice her watching him suspiciously.

REED: More milk? Or would you like some coffee?

MAURI: I'm fine, thanks.

He pours some for himself, returns to main room.

REED: So you've only just arrived?

MAURI: Yeah.

9

REED: How long will you be in the area? Do you know?

MAURI: Depends. I'll see how it goes.

>*He nods and moves to sit again. As he does, she has a brief coughing fit.*

REED: That doesn't sound too good.

MAURI: *(hoarse, clearing throat)* I'm okay.

REED: Have you been sick for a while?

MAURI: No, it just started today. I've had, like, chills. Sore throat.

REED: You might have the flu.

MAURI: Maybe.

REED: Do you—do you have a place to stay, Mauri? Around here?

MAURI: *(shrugs)* Don't worry about it.

REED: It's just that the rain is bad—and the wind…

MAURI: I can take care of myself. I've been on my own for a while.

REED: Can I ask how, um…how old you are?

MAURI: Almost sixteen.

REED: You don't—you don't live with your parents?

MAURI: *(scoffs)* No.

REED: I'm—sorry.

MAURI: *(looking around)* This is a nice place.

REED: I—like it.

MAURI: It's simple. I like simple things. And you're practically downtown.

REED: Yes.

MAURI: What do you do? I mean, like, your job?

REED: I work in a—a soup kitchen. "Meals for D.C.," it's called. "Medic," for short. I cook. I supervise in the kitchen.

MAURI: Really? I had you pegged for a scientist or a math teacher or something.

REED: *(smiles)* No.

MAURI: Good. 'Cause I suck at science *and* math.

REED: What *are* you good at, Mauri? In school.

MAURI: I used to be good at art. That's about it.

REED: English?

MAURI: I'm not into books. *(Stands, arms around herself, looks around)* You sure are, though.

REED: Well, I have a lot of time. My job isn't demanding.

MAURI: Wife? Kids?

REED: None.

MAURI: *(nods, interested)* Why not?

REED: I don't know.

MAURI: Are you gay?

11

REED: *(very embarrassed)* No, Mauri, I'm not gay.

MAURI: Are you sure? 'Cause it's totally cool if you are.

REED: I'm sure I'm not gay, Mauri.

MAURI: So why aren't you married? *(Coughs again. Sniffles. A shiver passes through her.)*

REED: Never met the right person, I guess. And I was—away. For a long time.

MAURI: Where?

REED: Just away.

MAURI: Army? Navy? Marines?

REED: Away.

MAURI: You weren't in a loony bin, were you?

>*They look at each other.*

MAURI: *(laughs suddenly)* Just messing with your head. *(She picks up a framed photo from a bookshelf, studies it.)* Your mom?

>*He stands, moves to her, takes the photo.*

REED: Yes. She died a long time ago.

MAURI: How about your dad?

REED: He's dead, too.

MAURI: *(looking)* You don't have a picture of him?

REED: No.

MAURI: What did you mean when you said you'd been away for a long time?

REED: *(shaking his head)* Nothing. I didn't mean anything. Can I get you something more to eat?

MAURI: No, I'm great, thanks.

REED: Well—how about you? Can I ask—?

MAURI: What?

REED: *(smiles)* Your hair.

MAURI: *(touches hair; self-conscious)* Don't you like it?

REED: I didn't say that. It's…*(lost for words; smiles, embarrassed)* What about your family?

MAURI: My family? Not much to tell there. Haven't seen them in a while.

REED: Are you—did you run away? Is that what you mean?

MAURI: *(casually)* Yeah.

REED: *(sits again)* I'm—sorry. To hear that.

MAURI: *(shrugs)* No big deal. *(Puts her hand to her forehead, sways slightly. Reed doesn't see.)*

REED: But to be without a family—that must be hard.

MAURI: It was harder being *with* one.

REED: Oh. Yes.

MAURI: I've lived in a lot of places since I left.

13

REED: Oh?

MAURI: I've been all around the country. West Coast to East.

REED: Looking for—that person? Who's not your friend? In all those places?

MAURI: No. The person I'm looking for is here. In the city.

REED: Well—I hope you find him. Him? Or her?

MAURI: *(sways again)* Mr. Waters?

REED: *(smiles)* I told you. 'Reed.'

MAURI: Reed, can I—where's the bathroom? I think I'm going to—

REED: *(realizing; jumps up)* Oh! Here, right here. *(Heads toward it, gestures.)*

> *She runs off to bathroom. Long pause. Reed finally turns back and stares at the spot near the fire where she had been sitting. After a moment he wanders over, picks up her plate and cup, takes them to the kitchen, glancing nervously toward the bathroom. He returns to the fire again, gives it a poke with a fireplace tool. He looks at her backpack sitting on the floor. It's unzipped and he takes a gingerly glance into it, not opening it, but simply placing one finger on the zipper and pushing slightly to try to get a glimpse of the bag's contents. He apparently doesn't see much. Sound of water running from direction of bathroom. He turns away, quickly and guiltily. Finally he moves toward the bathroom again.*

REED: Are you all right?

> *The response is an indistinct sound. After a moment she comes out, pale, shaken.*

14

MAURI: I threw up.

REED: Oh, Mauri, you must really be sick. I'm sorry.

MAURI: I think I'll go now.

> *She moves to the sofa, sits, begins pulling on her socks. Reed stands uncomfortably behind her, looking around, listening to the rain.*

REED: It's a bad night.

MAURI: I'll be okay.

REED: Do you—Mauri, do you have a place to stay? Really?

MAURI: I told you, don't worry about it.

REED: You're sure?

MAURI: I'm fine.

REED: Mauri, I've got a car. I could give you a ride someplace. Or maybe...do you need a doctor? I could drive you to the hospital.

MAURI: I'm all right. Stop worrying about me. *(Holds her head in her hands)* Shit, I think I'm going to throw up again. Wait. Wait...It's okay. I'm okay.

REED: Mauri, you're not okay. You're *not*.

MAURI: What do you care? You don't even know me. You have no idea who I am.

REED: No, but it's raining, and you're sick.

MAURI: I'm fine.

REED: You—could stay here.

MAURI: Here?

REED: Sure. The sofa you're sitting on folds out. It's not the greatest bed in the world, but it's a bed.

MAURI: You want me to stay here?

REED: You could. For tonight.

MAURI: Why?

REED: *(unsure)* No one should be left out in the rain.

> *She looks at him carefully, shakes her head and starts pulling on her shoes.*

MAURI: I don't think so.

> *He watches her silently. When she has the first shoe partly on she stops, holds her hands to her head. She is breathing hard, shivering, sweating.*

MAURI: Just let me— *(Coughing fit. After it passes she falls sideways on the sofa.)* Oh, shit.

> *Reed sits on the arm of the sofa.*

REED: You can't leave tonight, Mauri. Please. You'll be perfectly safe here.

MAURI: *(weakly)* Will I?

REED: Yes.

MAURI: No, I...I've got to go...

REED: I don't think you have anywhere to go.

MAURI: I'm all right...

16

REED: You're not all right.

MAURI: *(drifting)* You might…you might hurt me…

REED: I won't hurt you, Mauri.

MAURI: But you've hurt…others…

REED: Others?

MAURI: You've hurt other…people…everybody *(fading)*…hurts people…

REED: I won't hurt you, Mauri.

MAURI: I hurt someone…I did…Steven…oh my God…I…Steven…

REED: Shhh.

MAURI: I hurt…someone….

REED: Shhh.

MAURI: And you…you were—I know…what you did…

REED: *(very surprised)* What I did?

> *He studies her.*

REED: Mauri, why were you crying outside?

MAURI: Cry…?

REED: It was so strange. I woke up from a nightmare—there was crying in it. The phone rang. And when I came out here, I heard *you* crying. It was a terrible sound. Why were you crying?

MAURI: I…

She falls silent. She is too weak to resist when he takes her feet, removing the shoe, and tucks them onto the sofa.

MAURI: No…

He takes the throw from the sofa, unfolds it, drapes it over her.

REED: It's all right, Mauri. Everything is all right. Just go to sleep. You're safe here.

MAURI: Safe…

REED: Shhh. Shhh.

She has fallen asleep. He studies her. After a few moments he shuts the lights off in the main room and exits to bedroom. Rain fades.

Scene Two

The next morning. Mauri is on sofa as before, lightly snoring. Reed enters from bedroom, dressed plainly: jeans, T-shirt. Socks, no shoes. He checks on her briefly before looking at his watch, going to kitchen, pouring coffee which is already made. As he rummages about, she stirs.

MAURI: Mm—? What—?

REED: *(from kitchen)* Good morning.

She frowns perplexedly; sits up, looks around, orienting herself. She is sleepy, stiff, still not feeling very well.

REED: Are you feeling better?

MAURI: Did I sleep here all night?

REED: Yes, you did. I came out a couple of times to check on you, and I thought about waking you up so I could fold out the bed, but you looked so peaceful that I—well, I didn't.

MAURI: Is that coffee I smell?

REED: Yes, I came out a little while ago and got it started. Want some?

MAURI: Yeah, I do. Thanks. *(As he gets it she stands, looks about.)* I don't remember that much about last night.

REED: You were sick.

MAURI: I remember you bringing me in and giving me something to eat. *(Glances at him)* We didn't have sex, did we?

REED: *(blanches)* No. No, of course not. You just ate something and then fell asleep on the sofa there.

19

MAURI: Wow. Sorry about that. I don't usually fall asleep on random guys' sofas.

REED: *(with cup)* Cream? Sugar? *(Gestures to containers on counter)*

MAURI: Black, thanks. *(Takes cup, drinks)*

REED: How are you feeling?

MAURI: Like I could sleep for a month. The coffee helps.

REED: I'll make you breakfast.

MAURI: I'm okay. My stomach doesn't feel that great. *(Gestures to fruit bowl)* Can I just have one of these?

REED: Of course.

> *Mauri takes a piece of fruit, starts to eat it.*

REED: Your stomach hurts?

MAURI: Kind of. I threw up last night, didn't I?

REED: I'm afraid so.

MAURI: Yeah, I remember that now. Shit. I'm sorry.

REED: Don't be. It's—don't be.

> *Pause, awkward on Reed's part.*

MAURI: I'll get my crap together in a minute and get out of here, Mr. Waters. Hey, see, I remember your name, too.

REED: So you do. But call me Reed. And you're Mauri.

MAURI: Right.

REED: *(ill at ease; goes to window)* It should be a pretty day. Clear. Not too cold. *(She doesn't respond.)* Mauri, I have a friend coming over shortly.

MAURI: Okay. I'll scram.

REED: No, I didn't mean that. You don't have to leave.

MAURI: I think I'd better.

REED: Actually he's about your age. A year or two older. His name is Will. Will Bliss. I help him with school things. We're friends. I'm driving him to a library this morning for a school project of his.

MAURI: You're like his tutor? That's cool.

REED: What I mean is—you wouldn't have to go. You could stay here. While we were gone.

MAURI: What would I do here?

REED: *(smiles)* Sleep for a month?

> She laughs. The fruit and coffee have brightened her.

MAURI: Here, huh?

REED: Why not?

MAURI: Well, you might attack me or something.

REED: I didn't attack you last night.

MAURI: *(thoughtfully)* No, you didn't.

REED: I'm serious. You could stay. For a while.

21

MAURI: I don't know you, Reed. Maybe you have some deep, dark past. Maybe you're hiding all kinds of things you don't want anyone to know about.

REED: You'd be perfectly safe here, Mauri. Just until you—you could decide what to do. Until you find your person.

MAURI: Person?

REED: The one you told me you were looking for.

MAURI: Oh. Him. I suspect he won't be hard to find.

> *Pause.*

REED: Maybe you'd like to take a shower?

MAURI: You mean with you?

REED: *(very embarrassed)* No. Not with me. Please—please stop saying things like that. That's not what I mean. I just meant—

MAURI: Oh. I gotcha. Well, yeah. That would be great. If it's okay.

REED: Of course it is. I'll get you a towel.

> *Reed heads off toward bathroom. Mauri turns,*
> *notices a few dollars on the counter, picks them*
> *up, rapidly counts them. Strips two bills away*
> *and puts them in her pocket. Reed returns.*
> *Outside, Will appears and heads toward the*
> *front door.*

REED: Here you are. You remember where the bathroom is, right?

> *He hands her the towel. She lingers.*

MAURI: You know—we *could* do that.

REED: What?

MAURI: What I said before. About the shower.

> *She touches him. They look at each other a long, tense moment. He seems both attracted and repelled.*

REED: Mauri, who—?

> *Will knocks on front door.*

REED: *(pulling away)* That's Will.

MAURI: Okay. I'll get myself clean. *(Exits toward bathroom)*

> *Reed, perturbed, goes to the door, opens it.*

REED: Will!

WILL: My man! *(Enters with backpack over his shoulder)* Whassup?

REED: Nothing much. *(trying to be hearty, but nervous; glancing back toward bathroom)* Are you ready for some hard research today?

WILL: That's what I'm talkin' about. "The Nature of Violence in Richard Wright." "Native Son." "Black Boy." Senior thesis. I'm all over it, dude. Ready to crack those real books.

REED: Good. Those small objects with the paper in them, right?

WILL: I've heard about 'em. Looking forward to making their acquaintance.

REED: Well, I'm about ready. Why don't we go?

WILL: Aw, you're forgetting something, though.

REED: What's that?

WILL: *(smiles)* You're getting old, man. Absent-minded.

REED: What am I forgetting?

WILL: *(Hums main theme from Tchaikovsky's 1st Piano Concerto)*

REED: Oh! You're right, I completely forgot! *(Goes to bookshelf, looks through CDs)* I've got it here somewhere. I'm sure of it.

WILL: Be great if you could loan it to me. I'll rip it and get the disc back to you next time.

REED: Well, there's certainly no hurry…Where is it, anyway? I could have sworn…Maybe I could find it for you next time. We should probably go.

WILL: What's the hurry? *(He drops himself into a chair)* Those ol' books will wait, I'll bet. They won't run away.

REED: Well, it's not that, it's just…Oh, here it is. *(Pulls out a CD, brings it to Will)* This is it. I think you'll like it.

WILL: *(taking it)* Cool. *(reading the back)* "Piano Concerto Number One, Op. 23." Reed, what's "Op." again?

REED: *(still nervous)* "Opus." It's the number of the work. So the Piano Concerto is Tchaikovsky's twenty-third piece of music. I think we should…

WILL: *(reading)* "Allegro non troppo." "Allegro con spirito." Damn.

REED: It's just in Italian. It means…

WILL: No wonder my family thinks I'm crazy for listening to this crap. Not even in English. Why don't they translate it?

REED: Well—actually, that's a good question—
> *Mauri re-enters hurriedly, wearing nothing but the towel Reed gave her. She moves quickly to her backpack.*

24

MAURI: Sorry—forgot my stuff. *(As she takes the backpack, she glances at Will and smiles)* Hi! *(Exits quickly)*

> *Long pause. Will is shocked, but not really judgmental. The moment should be played lightly.*

WILL: Reed, what the hell was *that?*

REED: *(he has turned away, deeply embarrassed)* It's not what you think, Will.

WILL: I didn't say what I thought.

REED: She's a runaway. She ran away from home. I gave her a place to sleep last night. *(Pointing)* On the sofa.

WILL: *(thoughtful)* How'd you meet her?

> *Sound of water from bathroom.*

REED: She was camping on the lawn outside. I heard her crying.

WILL: Crying?

> *Reed nods.*

WILL: Hm. How about that.

REED: She was...sick. I think she still is. She all but passed out last night.

WILL: Know where she's from?

REED: *(shakes his head)* She didn't say.

> *Pause.*

WILL: Well, this is an awkward development.

REED: Will, I swear to you. I just gave her a meal and—

WILL: *(ironically; he believes Reed, but can't resist teasing him)* It's your business, Reed. Got yourself a little love nest here, a few little hotties on the side, it's all good. Never figured you for a player, though. Got any more hiding in the bedroom?

REED: *No. (realizing Will is kidding)* Come on, Will. I feel strange enough about this as it is.

WILL: You ought to, man. Not every day I see chicks running around in towels in here. Maybe I just haven't been coming at the right times.

REED: Will...

WILL: Got any sloppy seconds for me, Reed? That one looked pretty fine. Good taste.

Reed shakes his head, laughs.

WILL: What's she going to do?

REED: I—don't know.

WILL: Well, be careful. She might rip off everything you have.

REED: *(shrugs)* I don't have much. And I don't think she'll stay. She just came in out of the rain, that's all. Came in out of the rain like a—stray cat.

WILL: An under-aged stray cat, looks like.

REED: Yes, I—that crossed my mind. Will, I think she's in some trouble. I'm not sure what's going on with her.

WILL: It's not your job to take care of some random girl, Reed.

REED: I know, but...Well, I'm sure she'll go soon. And so will we. To the library. Richard Wright, right?

26

WILL: Right.

REED: Want something to drink? While we're waiting?

WILL: Sure.

> *During the following dialogue they go to kitchen, Reed gets glasses, pours soda or juice from refrigerator, gives Will a glass.*

WILL: Reed, why do you live like this, man? I don't get it. I never have.

REED: Like what?

WILL: This. I mean, no offense, but come on. You're the smartest guy I know. Why do you live in this little place? Why do you work in a stupid-ass soup kitchen?

REED: Come on, Will. Don't call my job "stupid-ass."

WILL: Sorry. But you know what I mean. You've read everything. You speak different languages. You could do a lot of things, man.

REED: Well, I feed the homeless. That's something, isn't it?

WILL: Man, you should be running that place down there.

REED: *(smiles)* I'm glad you think so.

WILL: You haven't done work like that your whole life, have you? Cooking and stuff? You've done other things.

REED: Oh, sure. I've been a bartender, short-order cook. I've worked on a ranch, I've picked apples. I even drove a tomato truck.

WILL: Why? Why little jobs like that?

REED: Some people just aren't ambitious, Will. We can't all be like you— you and your public relations career.

WILL: I don't even know if you have a college degree. Do you?

REED: No. I went for a year, a long time ago.

WILL: What happened?

REED: I—I had to go away. Something—something came up.

Sound of water ceases.

WILL: Sounds like your little friend's done in there. So you never went back? To college?

REED: I never went back.

WILL: That's too bad. You should've.

REED: Maybe.

WILL: You still could. What's to stop you?

REED: No, it's too late for me. But *you'll* finish.

WILL: If I ever get started.

REED: Are you kidding? With your grades? Any university would be lucky to have you.

WILL: Those universities cost money, last I heard. There's nothing at home. My mom can't help. A waitress? With five kids? And obviously Dad isn't around.

REED: There are scholarships.

WILL: Have to be some damn good ones.

REED: Will, we had this same conversation the day we met. Remember?

WILL: In the music section of that big bookstore downtown. Yeah.

28

REED: You were looking for—

WILL: Beethoven. *(Hums the opening of the "Eroica" Symphony)*

REED: You were humming it for the clerk. But she had no idea.

WILL: *(imitating Reed)* "Excuse me? I couldn't help overhearing, young man. That's the opening to Beethoven's 'Eroica' Symphony." We ended up in their little café, talking about music for—what? An hour?

REED: At least. And other things, too.

WILL: What was that? Like, a year ago, now.

REED: And you were saying the same things then. About college.

WILL: Yeah, well—nothing's changed.

REED: Will, you'll do fine. Keep up on the paperwork. Bring me more of those applications, like you did before. I'll help you with them.

WILL: Well, thanks.

REED: In the meantime—

> *Mauri appears, barefoot in a different T-shirt*
> *than before, the same jeans. She is rubbing a*
> *towel to her damp hair.*

MAURI: Hey.

REED: Feeling better?

MAURI: Yeah, a little. I keep getting the shivers, though. I turned up the water as hot as it would go.

REED: Something to drink?

MAURI: I'm okay. I guess I should leave.

REED: Where are you going?

MAURI: *(shrugs)* Wherever.

REED: To find your—person? *(to Will)* She came to the city to find someone, she told me.

WILL: Oh yeah? Where did you come from?

MAURI: Lots of places.

WILL: And you just got here?

MAURI: Yeah. Yesterday.

REED: I found her under my window outside.

WILL: Going to stay long?

MAURI: I don't know yet.

WILL: It's a nice city. Parts of it, anyway. And most things are free. Museums and things.

MAURI: Yeah, I wouldn't mind seeing some of that stuff. *(Drops into a chair)*

REED: Mauri, I have an idea.

MAURI: What's that?

REED: Why don't you—why don't you stay here while Will and I go to the library? Get some more rest. Relax. Have something to eat, watch TV. Sleep if you want. Then when we get back maybe the three of us could go out for a meal. How would that be?

MAURI: *(studies Reed)* I don't want to get in the way.

REED: Will? Is it all right?

WILL: *(shrugs)* Sure, cool. Whatever. It's your show, man.

MAURI: Well…I don't have any money for eating at restaurants and stuff like that.

REED: Oh, don't worry about that. Really. It's perfectly fine.

> *Pause.*

MAURI: Well…If you're sure you don't mind.

REED: It would be my pleasure. *Our* pleasure. Okay, that's settled. Let me just get my shoes, Will, and we'll go, all right?

WILL: Cool.

> *Reed exits. Mauri sits picking at her nails as Will studies her.*

WILL: So where do you go to school?

> *Mauri scoffs.*

WILL: What?

MAURI: Sorry, dude. I haven't been in school for a while now.

WILL: Really?

MAURI: Nope.

WILL: Why—I mean, why not?

> *She shrugs.*

WILL: You—you think you'll be here for a while? In the city?

MAURI: Maybe.

WILL: You have a place to stay?

MAURI: Not really. *(thumb in the direction of where Reed exited)* He keeps trying to get me to stay here. Probably for the usual reasons.

WILL: Nah. He's not like that.

MAURI: They're all like that. *You're* all like that.

WILL: Really. He's not. I've known him for a year now. There's nothing weird here. He doesn't even have any kiddie porn on his laptop. I've checked. *(Mauri chuckles.)* You could…

MAURI: What?

WILL: Well, what I mean is…*(Comes closer to her)* If you stayed around, I could maybe, you know, take you some places. I know the city pretty well. Lived here all my life.

MAURI: Are you asking me out? Like on a date?

WILL: Well…We can call it something else if you want.

> Mauri suddenly laughs, seemingly far more
> boisterously than Will's line warrants.

WILL: Well, forget it then—

MAURI: No—no, that's not why I'm laughing. I'm sorry. That's not what I meant at all. Sure, Will, if you want to show me the sights, and I'm around, sure. That'd be cool. Great.

WILL: Well, okay, then.

MAURI: But nothing where we have to dress up. This is about all I've got.

WILL: Nah, don't worry about it. It's cool. *(smiles)* But I liked your other outfit better.

32

MAURI: Other outfit?

WILL: You looked good in that towel.

MAURI: Oh yeah?

WILL: Only thing wrong with that outfit was the towel.

MAURI: *(smiles)* You're gonna be that way, huh?

WILL: I'll be any way you want me to be.

Reed enters, having put on his shoes.

REED: Well! Will, are you ready?

WILL: Sure thing, man. *(Gathers up his backpack)*

REED: *(privately, away from Will)* Mauri, you'll stay, then? Until we get back?

MAURI: Sure. If that's what you want.

REED: Well, if you *want* to leave, just please lock the door on your way out. But I hope that you don't. Leave, I mean.

MAURI: How do you know I won't rip you off while you're gone?

REED: *(smiles)* Mauri, there's nothing in here of any value. If you want something, just tell me. I'll give it to you.

MAURI: The shirt off your back?

REED: Well, if that's what you wanted, I'd buy you a new shirt.

MAURI: Okay.

REED: *(to Will)* Off to the palaces of education with us, young man.

WILL: You got it. *(Reed and Will cross to door)* Nice to meet you, Mauri.

MAURI: *(nods)* Have a nice time.

WILL: Nice, no. Necessary, yes. *(Exits)*

REED: 'Bye, Mauri. Take it easy, okay? Really. Get some rest. And…and you should put some socks on. *(Exits)*

> *Mauri is left alone in the apartment. After a long moment she stands, drapes her towel over a chair, looks about curiously. When she is alone whatever animation that has been lighting her face disappears and she appears lost, fearful. She looks at the items on the bookshelves, perhaps noses around in a drawer or two in the kitchen. Finally she goes to her backpack, brings out socks, puts them aside. Then she finds her bottle of alcohol, pulls it out, opens it, takes a long swig, looking about as if suspicious that someone will see her. She puts it away again. As she does, she espies another item in the backpack and brings it forth.*
>
> *It is a switchblade. She drops onto the sofa and studies it carefully for a moment. She pushes the button which causes the blade to flip open. She studies the blade for a long time, holding it close to her face, fascinated with it. Finally she extends her other arm, palm up, and places the blade lengthwise across her wrist. She plays with the blade against the softness of her skin, moving it this way and that, taking the point and pushing it into her wrist hard enough to make her gasp. Blackout.*

Scene Three

Evening, several days later. The apartment is empty. Mauri and Will are outside, fast-food soft drink cups in their hands from which they occasionally drink with straws. Mauri's clothing has noticeably improved—she wears a new top with perhaps a new belt, hat, shoes. She occasionally sniffles or rubs her nose.

MAURI: Thanks for the tour, Will. That was fun.

WILL: Well, there's a lot more to see in the city. We haven't even started. Some of the museums are actually interesting.

MAURI: I liked the dinosaurs.

WILL: Natural History's good, yeah. We could go to Air and Space next time. Look at spaceships.

MAURI: Yeah, okay, I guess. I'm not used to this much education, though. You make me feel like I'm on a school field trip.

WILL: Well, we don't have to do museums. There's...

MAURI: No, it's cool. Whatever. I don't care what I do.

WILL: You look good doing it, though. *(She scoffs)* Really. You've got some nice stuff on.

MAURI: Reed got me these things. I sure couldn't have afforded them.

WILL: He's like that. I have to stop him from buying me things sometimes.

MAURI: Where's he get his money, anyway? It can't be from working in that soup kitchen.

WILL: I don't know. I don't ask.

35

MAURI: You were right, though. It's totally cool there. I've been there almost a week and he doesn't, you know, make any false moves. He's nice. It's sort of weird.

WILL: That's just the way he is.

MAURI: He, like, nursed me, you know? I'm okay now, but I was really sick for a couple of days. He let me sleep on that fold-out sofa, he brought me chicken soup and boxes of Kleenex and shit like that. I mean, he doesn't even know me.

WILL: You been there a week, he's starting to know you.

MAURI: Yeah, I guess. Maybe I'm not what he thinks I am, though.

WILL: What do you mean?

MAURI: Nothing. Just—nobody's exactly what they seem, right? Maybe I'm not what you think I am, either. Maybe he's not what you think *he* is. *(Short pause)* Maybe you're not what I think *you* are, either.

WILL: If you think I'm a good-looking, brilliant young black man, then I guess I'm what you think I am.

MAURI: *(smiling)* I don't know much about you besides that, though. Your mom's a waitress. You've got four brothers and sisters. What about your dad? Is he in the picture?

WILL: He's dead.

MAURI: Aw, I'm sorry.

WILL: Died when I was seven. I don't remember him that well. But I remember him. He was a musician.

MAURI: Classical? Is that why you're into—?

WILL: No, no. Blues. He played guitar in a blues band. They were pretty good, too. They played a lot of gigs around the city. Sometimes in other places. I remember they took a trip to Philadelphia once, to play at some jazz festival there. I used to have a tape of them—you know, one of those old cassettes? Meant to put it on a disc sometime but now I can't find it. I can still hear it in my head, though. The songs. And I still see some of the guys who were in the band around the neighborhood. Don't know if they still do music.

MAURI: What would your dad think of all your classical stuff?

WILL: Dad? *(Smiles)* He'd think I was crazy, like everybody does. He taught me a few chords on the guitar. Wanted me to do blues when I grew up, rhythm and blues.

MAURI: How did he die?

WILL: *(Flatly)* Got shot.

MAURI: That's fucked up, Will. I'm sorry.

> *Will shrugs. They drink their sodas.*

WILL: What about you? How did you end up here, anyway?

MAURI: That's a long story, Will.

WILL: I got time.

MAURI: Not that much time. *(Sighs)* I grew up in California. Dad left. Mom married a guy who—we didn't get along. So I left.

WILL: How long ago?

MAURI: About…a year.

WILL: Been on the road ever since?

MAURI: Yeah.

WILL: How do you make enough money to live? You get jobs?

MAURI: Yeah, sort of. I live pretty cheap.

WILL: What kind of—I mean, what kind of life is that? Are you going to finish school?

MAURI: I don't know. I doubt it. What do you care, anyway? Is it your business?

WILL: Hey, okay. Forget it.

MAURI: Aw, shit. Will, I'm sorry. It's just—I don't do that well with questions about—you know, the future.

WILL: You live in the moment.

MAURI: Yeah, something like that. I mean, I think about it. I know I've got to make up my mind about some stuff.

WILL: Like…?

MAURI: *(shrugs)* You know. How long I'm going to stay around here, for one thing.

WILL: Well, I—I hope you stay a long time.

> *Pause.*

MAURI: Gimme your hand. *(He does.)* Want me to read your palm?

WILL: I don't believe in that stuff.

MAURI: I know how. I'm serious. *(She studies his palm closely.)* See this? This is your lifeline. See how long it is? Straight and unbroken. You're going to have a long, healthy life.

WILL: How does my hand know that?

MAURI: I'm telling you, I read a book about it. And this—this is your love line...Uh-oh.

WILL: What?

MAURI: What've you been up to, Will?

WILL: What do you mean?

MAURI: I've never seen a love line like this.

WILL: What?

MAURI: Well—I can't tell you. It's too gruesome. It's *scandalous.*

WILL: Why?

MAURI: Do you really want to know?

WILL: Yes!

MAURI: Well, see this? Your love line? It hooks up over here, to this one. See?

WILL: What's that?

MAURI: That's—well, that's your phone sex line.

WILL: My...? *(laughs)*

MAURI: I'm telling you! It's a scientific fact! *(playing with his hand)* And here's your power line. See? And this is your laundry line. And this one's your fishing line.

WILL: Girl, I don't think you can see a damn thing about my future!

Both laughing, they grab at each other and wrestle playfully. Mauri breaks away. Will chases, catches and holds her. As their laughter begins to subside, they kiss. Afterward they look at each other, both of them clearly surprised by this development.

WILL: Wow.

MAURI: Yeah.

WILL: Um…

MAURI: Don't talk.

WILL: Mauri…

They kiss again.

MAURI: C'mon, let's go in.

WILL: Why don't we stay out here a while?

MAURI: It's getting cold.

WILL: I'll keep you warm.

MAURI: Oh, my God! You are so corny.

WILL: Mauri, I feel like—like I should tell you that—

MAURI: Don't. Don't say anything. Don't ruin it.

WILL: I just meant…

MAURI: Don't. Don't say the kind of stuff guys say when they're making out with girls. I don't want to hear it.

They hold each other.

WILL: I—

MAURI: Shh.

WILL: Mauri—

MAURI: Let's go in, Will. C'mon, let's go in. Please.

She leads him by the hand into the apartment.

MAURI: Reed! Are you home?

REED: *(offstage)* Yes!

WILL: Whassup, man?

Reed enters.

REED: Ah—you're back. Terrific. How was your day?

MAURI: Great.

REED: Good. Sit down, sit down. *(They sit.)* Mauri, how are you feeling?

MAURI: I'm fine, Reed. *(to Will)* He's always asking me how I am.

REED: Well, you were really sick. You had a temperature of a hundred and two. Are you sure you're okay? I know you're not completely over it yet.

MAURI: *(to Will)* See what I mean?

WILL: He's a regular mother hen.

REED: We should take your temperature again. Just to be sure.

MAURI: I'm *fine*, Reed.

REED: Well, if you say so. So what did you two kids do?

MAURI: Just messed around. Had some phone sex.

REED: What?

WILL: She's kidding, man. We—we went fishing.

REED: Mm. *(deadpan, glancing between them)* And were the fish—biting?

WILL: Got a nibble or two, yeah. *(He and Mauri laugh.)* Reed, we're just messing with your mind. We went downtown, saw some museums. That's all.

REED: Well, that's great.

MAURI: What about you?

WILL: Yeah, what about you? You raise some hell down there at that soup kitchen of yours?

REED: Actually, something strange happened. Or—well, *I* thought it was strange. *(Pause.)* They fired me.

WILL: *Fired* you!

REED: *(nodding, clearly puzzled)* Yes. They said they had too many people, they had to let some go.

WILL: But you practically run that dump down there, man. The kitchen, anyway.

REED: Yes, it's—odd. I don't understand it.

WILL: How long you been working there?

REED: A couple of years.

WILL: And they just fired you? Just like that?

42

REED: Just like that.

WILL: Damn. That sucks, man. Are you going to be okay? I mean—like, with money?

REED: *(slightly distracted)* Hm? Oh, yes, Will, there are no problems on that score. I never did that job for the money, not really.

WILL: Well, I'm glad to hear that.

REED: No, I—have some money. That's all right.

WILL: What'll you do?

REED: I—don't know. It's so strange. It seems like there must be something—something else to it. Something I don't understand.

WILL: Well, man, if you don't need the money, you know—it was just a kitchen job. No great loss.

REED: No, I guess not. But I liked the routine. *(Smiles weakly)* Gave me something to do.

WILL: You'll get another job easy, Reed. If you want one.

REED: Yes, I suppose.

> *Pause.*

WILL: *(standing)* Well, look, I'd better be getting home. Gotta watch the little siblings. Mom's shift starts in an hour.

REED: I could drive you.

WILL: Nah, I'm fine. The bus is right at the corner.

REED: *(standing; he and Will move to door)* Well, all right then. Take care. When are we working on that thesis?

43

WILL: Thursday? How's that?

REED: Okay. Great.

WILL: *(to Mauri, who has not moved)* Later, Mauri.

MAURI: Yeah, Will. Later. Thanks. I had a great time.

WILL: Right. *(Glances at Reed)* Later, man. Don't worry about it. It was a stupid-ass job anyway.
> Reed chuckles, swats at Will's head playfully.
> Will exits.

REED: He's a nice young man, isn't he?

> Mauri nods.

REED: Why so quiet?

MAURI: Hm? Oh. No reason. A little tired from all the walking we did, I guess.

REED: Are you ready for something to eat?

MAURI: We ate, Reed. Me and Will. I'm not hungry.

REED: Well…If you're sure.

MAURI: Yeah. Thanks.

REED: *(sits)* I still can't get over it. Just being let go like that.

MAURI: Well, don't worry about it. You said you've got money, right?

REED: It's not the money. It's…well, that was my first job in a long while.

MAURI: I can't believe you'd be unemployed for long. Somebody'd hire you to do something.

44

REED: Well, there were…other circumstances.

MAURI: That long time you were away that you told me about?

REED: Yes…yes.

MAURI: Where were you, anyway? During that time?

REED: Well…look, let's not talk about it, okay? It's not important anymore. Some tea?

MAURI: No, I'm okay, Reed. I was thinking, though, that maybe I should—you know, move on. Check out of this-here hotel.

REED: Why?

MAURI: You've done enough for me. Look at this stuff. *(Indicating the clothes she's wearing, other new clothes piled near sofa)* You bought me a lot. You need to stop buying me things. I don't like *owing* people.

REED: You don't owe me anything, Mauri.

MAURI: Yeah, that's what you say now. But sometime you'll get mad at me and say, 'What about all those clothes I bought you? What about my letting you stay in my apartment? And all the food? What about that?'

REED: I won't.

MAURI: You will. You'll get mad at me sooner or later if I stick around.

REED: Don't be silly. I enjoy having you here. I like the company. I mean, eventually you'll want to go back to your parents, I'm sure, but for now…

MAURI: My *parents?*

REED: Eventually.

MAURI: You want me to go back to *them?*

45

REED: Well, Mauri, I'm sure that whatever problems you have with them can be worked out. In time.

MAURI: By who? By you?

REED: No, not me. That's not what I meant.

MAURI: Oh, what do you know about it, anyway? You want to know something about my parents? My dad left when I was little. He's a college professor. He went off to a job at a college in northern California and moved in with a guy. Like, his boyfriend. They've been together now for ten years or something.

REED: That—well, that's...

MAURI: I was his little experiment in trying to be straight. Didn't work.

REED: That doesn't mean he doesn't love you. It...

MAURI: I haven't heard from my dad in, like, eight years. That's all over. You can imagine what it did to my mom. Well, she remarried a few years ago to a guy named James. James Dyson. He runs a construction company. And the two of them—they drink.

REED: Oh.

MAURI: I mean, they *drink*. And drinking makes them horny for each other.

REED: Mauri—

MAURI: They're always grinding on each other in the living room. It's disgusting. And she always claims I'm hot for James. She said it for years and years. Hot! For her big flabby disgusting husband! *(Pause)* I remember once, when they were first married, standing in the doorway to the living room and watching them slow dance together. Mom's blouse was all open and her...tits were all hanging out and he was pushing his, like, pelvis onto her. They both had drinks in their hands. She looked at me and said, 'I'll bet you wish he was doing this to you.' I was *eleven*.

46

REED: That's—awful.

MAURI: Yeah. James had other issues, too. He'd bump against me sometimes, when Mom wasn't home. Always when she wasn't home. He never grabbed me or anything like that. It was more like, when we passed each other in the hall he'd just happen to brush up against me. His hip against mine. Or when he was reaching for something in the kitchen his arm would just happen to bump against my chest. He did it again and again. It *wasn't* my imagination.

REED: I'm sure it wasn't.

MAURI: Yeah, well—that's my parents. I wish…

REED: What? What do you wish?

MAURI: Nothing, I guess. Nothing in particular. I just wish. *(Pause)* We lived on Bourne Street, you know? I started thinking of it as Mourn Street. You know, like you're in mourning? For somebody who died?

> *Pause.*

REED: Would you like me to start a fire?

MAURI: I'm okay. I'm not cold. Stop *doing* things for me, okay?

REED: I'm—sorry.

MAURI: And stop saying you're sorry. You're always saying that.

REED: I'm— *(Falls silent)*

MAURI: So I tell you all about myself, but you've got nothing to say.

REED: Well—I wish things were better with your parents, Mauri.

MAURI: No. Not that. I mean about you. You're still being this, like, mystery man.

47

REED: I'm not so mysterious.

MAURI: Really? What do I know about you? I mean, besides what I can see in this apartment? And that you're friends with Will? And that you work at a soup kitchen? Or did, I mean.

REED: There's not much to know. I'm a very boring person.

MAURI: I'm not so sure about that.

REED: Well... *(clearly reluctant)* I'm from California too, coincidentally.

MAURI: I don't believe in coincidences.

REED: No? What do you believe in?

MAURI: Fate.

REED: Really? Do you believe we were fated to meet?

MAURI: Maybe.

REED: Why do you think that is?

MAURI: You tell me.

REED: I haven't the slightest idea. I believe in coincidences, remember?

MAURI: Oh yeah. That's right.

REED: Anyway, I...I grew up in California. A little town called Satin.

MAURI: Never heard of it.

REED: No, you probably wouldn't have. It's a very small town. My mother died when I was young. I lived with my father. He ran an automobile dealership. He died too, eventually. But that was later.

MAURI: After your mysterious...going away?

48

REED: Um…During it. Actually.

MAURI: Were you in jail, Reed?

> *Reed is extremely uncomfortable with the direction this conversation has taken, but he is aware that because Mauri has shared personal confidences with him, he is expected to reciprocate. He moves away from her.*

REED: No. I wasn't in jail.

MAURI: Where, then?

> *Long pause.*

REED: I was in a…an institution. A…what you'd call a—an institution. A mental institution.

> *She nods slowly, listening.*

REED: I—

> *But the pain of this is overwhelming. He cannot continue talking. He drops down on the sofa, not looking at her.*

MAURI: It's okay, Reed.

REED: No. It's not.

MAURI: It's okay to tell me.

> *Pause.*

REED: I suppose you really want to leave now.

MAURI: Hm? Why?

REED: Now that you know I'm a—a crazy person. *(Pause.)* I wish I knew why they fired me. I wonder if…

MAURI: You're not crazy, Reed. Shit. *(Pause)* Why were you in there?

REED: In…?

MAURI: That place. That institution.

> *Long pause.*

REED: Are you sure you wouldn't like some tea?

MAURI: Okay, okay, never mind.

REED: I'm— *(Smiles)* I was going to say I'm sorry again.

MAURI: *(laughs)* You're not crazy, Reed, you're a dork.

REED: Well—

MAURI: You sure as shit don't need to be sensitive about anything around *me*.

REED: I guess you have a hard life, Mauri. It's got to be hard.

MAURI: Me? *(Shrugs)* I always get by somehow. Steal shit.

REED: Money?

MAURI: Yeah, I've stolen some in my time. But usually stuff from 7-Elevens and things like that. Food. Sometimes clothes. You'd be surprised how easy it is to steal a shirt out of a clothing store. Take it into the changing room, take off your old shirt, put the new one on, then put the old one on over it. Walk straight out of the store when the clerks are busy.

REED: I'll—remember that.

MAURI: You should. Your wardrobe could use some help, dude.

REED: Maybe I could take us both to a clothing store. You can pick some things out for yourself while we're at it.

MAURI: There you go again. *(Rises)* I told you, I don't want to *owe* you.

REED: Mauri, it's perfectly all right. I've got nothing to do with my money.

MAURI: Where do you get it, anyway? Your money?

REED: My—father. After he died. He left some.

MAURI: Why do you live in a shithole like this, then? I mean, no offense.

REED: I like it. And I'm not rich, you know. Not at all.

MAURI: *Money.* Seems like that's all that matters, sometimes.

REED: How do you get yours? Surely you don't steal *all* of it. You haven't stolen anything from me except for the ten dollars I had on the counter there. *(Gestures)*

MAURI: *(embarrassed)* Oh—shit. Um—yeah. Sorry about that. Here, I'll give it back— *(Reaches into her pocket)*

REED: No, no, that's not what I mean. You're welcome to it. Just tell me when you need some and I'll give it to you.

MAURI: An allowance?

REED: Well—something like that.

MAURI: *(shaking her head)* I don't get you, dude. I really don't. I mean, this is just weird. You take me in, you treat me like—like your daughter or something. What did I ever do for you?

REED: You—came in out of the rain.

51

MAURI: Okay. I'll give you one guess how I get my money. *(Gently mocking)* Now, let's see…teenage girl…runaway…no job skills…lives on the streets…Gee. *Hmmmmm.* I wonder what she does for money?

REED: That's what I was—afraid of.

MAURI: Not very surprising, huh?

REED: I'm just concerned about your health. It's not—

MAURI: Oh, I don't do anything that would get me an STD. I mean, not a really *bad* one, at least. Just quick things in cars, shit like that. I can make thirty, forty bucks in five minutes. It keeps me in Twinkies, at least.

REED: Mauri, it's so dangerous, that kind of thing.

MAURI: I know. Maybe I'll get lucky some night and a guy will strangle me or something.

REED: Do you think you'd like that?

MAURI: Sometimes I do. *(Moves close to him)* So now you know.

REED: Yes.

MAURI: So if you want me to, you know, earn my rent around here, I'm willing to do it. It's fine.

REED: I don't want you to earn your rent, Mauri.

MAURI: *(sudden mood swing)* Then what *do* you want, man? Maybe I should just go. *(Moves to gather her things.)*

REED: No, Mauri, don't.

MAURI: Fuck it. Fuck *this*. This is too weird for me.

REED: What is?

52

MAURI: You. This whole thing. Weird guy from a mental institution taking care of the little street whore. If you were *fucking* me, I'd understand. But this...

REED: Mauri, stop. You're being silly. Just stop.

MAURI: Just leave me alone!

> *Pause.*

REED: Mauri, you're welcome to stay here. For as long as you like. Because I like you. Will likes you. Other than him, I never have company. I have no relatives. I know no one. I...There's no problem here, that's all. Just... just stay. Just...

> *This short speech deflates Mauri. She stops collecting her belongings, remains motionless.*

MAURI: You like me?

REED: Yes.

MAURI: Really?

REED: Yes.

> *After a moment Mauri begins to giggle. The giggle grows slowly to full-out laughter. The laughter takes on a hysterical tone as the lights black out.*

Scene Four

Some days later. Reed is discovered at the phone, a broom in his hand. Mauri can be heard offstage, in the bathroom, singing or humming.

REED: Hello, Will? I keep getting your answering machine…I think this is the third message I've left. Are you all right? You missed our appointment to work on your project and I haven't heard a word from you in nearly a week…I sent you an e-mail, too. Well… Let me hear from you as soon as you get this message, okay?

He hangs up, resumes sweeping the kitchen. After a moment he finishes. Then he wipes the countertop. Seeing that the front room is in some disarray with Mauri's things lying about, he begins to pick them up. He gingerly picks up a bra lying on the floor and drops it into her backpack. Then he folds a shirt. Finally he picks up her jeans, which are crumpled in a corner. As he does, a piece of paper flutters out of them. He bends to pick it up: a news clipping. Curiously, he unfolds it. What he sees leaves him speechless. He drops the pants, stares at the paper. Glances back toward the bathroom, his face almost panic-stricken.

REED: Oh my God.

Stares at the paper a moment longer. Then, glancing back toward the bathroom again, he gathers up her pants and returns the paper to the pocket. He folds the pants and leaves them neatly stacked with the shirt. He sits down then—virtually collapses.

Mauri appears, in a bright mood.

MAURI: Hey, Reed, you know what I need to get? There are these skin pads I like to use when my face is breaking out. Which it's doing now. Maybe we could go to a drugstore today. They usually have them. *(She crosses to kitchen, looks into refrigerator.)* You know, we need to buy some food. I mean, there's like nothing in here. Some milk. Cheese. *(She looks around in kitchen cabinets.)* Look at this. I mean, what are we, monks or something? Bread...Oatmeal...Boring! We should do a shopping trip. I want some cereal. Not that crappy fiber stuff you buy, either. *Real* cereal. Cap'n Crunch. Cocoa Puffs. And Pop Tarts. Chocolate Pop Tarts. *(Turns from the kitchen in frustration, partly feigned.)* Maybe we should just go to McDonalds. How about that? I could do a Big Mac. Huh? What do you say, Reed? Should we go out and get some *real* food?

> *She realizes that he is not responding. She moves to him.*

MAURI: Reed?

> *Looks at him for a long moment, sees in his face that something serious has happened.*

MAURI: Reed, what is it? *(She drops down next to him.)* Are you okay?

REED: Yes, I'm...okay.

MAURI: Why so quiet? What's wrong?

REED: Am I?

MAURI: What?

REED: Quiet.

MAURI: Yeah. You are. *(Pause)* Are you mad at me?

REED: No.

MAURI: Because I'm such a slob? Is that it? I'll pick up this stuff, I promise.

REED: I'm not mad at you.

MAURI: Something's wrong.

> *Pause. She drops her head onto his shoulder.*

MAURI: Do you want some tea?

REED: How is your mother, Mauri?

MAURI: What?

REED: Your mother.

MAURI: My mother?

REED: Yes. How is she?

MAURI: I don't know how she is. I haven't talked to her in months. You know that.

REED: Oh, yes. Of course.

MAURI: What is this? Why are you asking about her?

REED: I just wondered.

MAURI: Wondered what? Wondered why?

REED: Well…it's been a long time since I've seen her.

MAURI: *Seen* her? Reed, what the hell's wrong with you?

REED: About…ten years, I think. *(Pause.)* Yes, about ten years. Maybe eleven. I remember her well. She attended every day of the trial. After all, I did murder her sister. *(Pause)* That would be your aunt.

> *She stares at him, wide-eyed, and slides away*
> *from him on the sofa. But she does not stand.*

56

MAURI: How did you find out?

REED: There was a news clipping in the pocket of your jeans. If you'd only been tidier, I wouldn't have seen it at all.

Pause.

MAURI: *(small smile)* I guess that means I should be tidier.

REED: *(smiling thinly)* You don't look a thing like Evie, you know. Or like Dorothy, either.

MAURI: People always said I look like my dad.

REED: Your name is Dyson, not Stevens.

MAURI: Yeah.

REED: You didn't just happen to come in out of the rain that night.

MAURI: No.

REED: Why did you come here? What do you want?

Mauri stands.

MAURI: I don't know.

REED: It couldn't have been that easy to locate me.

MAURI: It was easier than you think.

REED: And you came all the way from California…

MAURI: Yeah. Took some detours, but yeah.

REED: You must have been very young when I…did what I did.

MAURI: I was five.

REED: You know, I always wondered what you meant. That first night.

MAURI: Hm?

REED: When you were so sick, when you were falling asleep here on the sofa, you said, 'I know what you did.'

MAURI: I said that?

REED: Yes. Very strange. You were ill. I always wondered why you said that, what you were talking about. You said I'd hurt someone.

MAURI: I don't remember that.

REED: No, you wouldn't. You slept for a long time right after. You said that *you* hurt someone, too.

MAURI: I did?

REED: Yes. You said the name 'Steven' again and again.

MAURI: No, I didn't. I didn't say that.

REED: You did. Maybe you were…delirious.

MAURI: Yeah. Maybe.

REED: 'I know what you did,' you said.

MAURI: So why didn't you just ask me? The next day? What I meant?

REED: Maybe I was afraid of the answer. And then—and then we just started getting along, you moved in…

MAURI: Yeah.

REED: I forgot about it. Or I tried to. I thought of it now and then. And that's why, when I found the clipping from the newspaper, I wasn't surprised, somehow. Shocked. Not surprised.

MAURI: Yeah. Well.

Pause. Reed puts his head in his hands.

REED: Why did you come here?

MAURI: You have no right to ask me any questions.

REED: Well—you've been living here for the past couple of weeks—

MAURI: See? I knew you'd bring that up when you got mad at me. I *told* you you would.

REED: I'm not mad.

MAURI: Oh, bullshit. Bullshit liar.

REED: Mauri—

MAURI: You don't know what my life's been like. You have *no* idea.

REED: I—

MAURI: Do you want to know why I ran away?

REED: You told me—about your stepfather, and…

MAURI: Shit. That was nothing. I didn't run away because of him. Well, not completely. I got involved with a guy when I was fourteen. Alan. He was older, like seventeen. We used to drive around at night. He'd take me up into the foothills, up Mulholland Drive. Sometimes we'd go into Hollywood, cruise up and down Sunset Boulevard. It was cool. Or—I thought it was. Well, one night he took me to this bad neighborhood in Pacoima. I kept asking him, 'Why are we here? Why?' He kept telling me it was okay. He pulled up in front of this old abandoned house. I didn't want to go in. But I did. He said we'd have fun. Turned out there were a bunch of his—friends there. It was a gang thing. He was being initiated. I—I was the initiation. *(Pause)*

59

MAURI (cont'd): There were six of them. It went on a long time. One of them held his hand tight over my face, so tight that I—I could—could barely breathe...I remember how at the end I was just laying there hoping they'd kill me. Just kill me. But they didn't. One of them, though, as they were leaving, one of them turned around and looked at me and spit at me. I remember seeing it arc down toward me, then it hit my cheek. That was the worst of it. Worse than the other. Sometimes I still think I can feel that spit on my cheek. Well—I got dressed, somehow. What was left of my clothes. I kept thinking they'd come back, they'd come back to kill me, but no. I was alone in the house. I pulled some stuff on and staggered out the door—I was bleeding, my arms were scratched up. I tried to figure out how to get home. I found a bus stop—I actually had a couple of dollars in my pocket still. They hadn't even bothered to rob me. I got home, finally. I was late. Nobody was there. I took a long shower. The longest shower of my life. I napped for an hour or two. Then I packed up my shit and left. That was it. I left.

*Reed stands, moves to her, motions as if he wants
to put his arms around her, but stops.*

MAURI: I had a lot of time to think. It was like, my life went to shit a long time ago. The more I thought about it, the more I realized that I'd only been really happy when Evie was alive. She was more like a mother to me than my mother had been. I remember her hair—it went almost to her waist—and these big hoop earrings she would wear. She had this big laugh, like a, what do they call it, a horse laugh. She was always taking care of me when Mom wasn't around. She lived with us for a while. She took me places. We would go shopping, to kid's places. Aunt Evie. We were close. Really, really close. I always used to wish that she'd been my mother. I even used to think sometimes that if Mom would just die, then Evie could adopt me and I'd be happy forever. But that was before...Well. Finding you wasn't really that hard. I knew where they'd put you, in that mental hospital up north. Mom kept tabs on you, believe me. She had all the news clippings, with your picture and stuff. And she was always talking to our lawyer, Mr. Perrywinkle. I bet you remember him too.

REED: I remember him.

MAURI: Well, I went up there. Took a bus. Walked right in the front door. It was weird, thinking that you were so close. That maybe if I just turned a corner I'd run right into you. I don't know what I wanted. I just wanted to—to *see*, I guess. To see this person who fucked up my life and who probably didn't even know that I existed.

REED: I—knew. I knew Dorothy had a child.

MAURI: So I walk up to the front desk and ask for you. I tell them I'm your long-lost daughter. Well, the lady at the desk looks up something on her computer and says, 'I'm sorry, but he's been discharged.' That was news to me. I asked where you'd gone and she just said they didn't give out that kind of information. Then a weird thing happened. I had to pee, so I asked where the bathroom was. I went in, did my thing, came back out, and noticed that my shoe was untied. As I reached down, I realized that I could hear the lady talking to someone around the corner. This person was saying, like, 'What *did* become of Reed Waters, anyway?' And the other lady said, 'He moved to the Washington, D.C. area, I think.' That was it. I finished tying my shoe and left. After that it was easy. Your phone number isn't even unlisted.

REED: It took you—a year? To find me?

MAURI: No. There were other—complications. Never mind that. *(Sudden change of mood)* Oh God, why did you kill Evie? Why would anyone kill Evie? How could you have hated her that much?

REED: I—didn't. Hate her. I—I loved her.

> *Mauri turns, glares furiously at him.*

MAURI: How dare you say that. How *dare* you say that shit to me. You *murdered* her!

REED: It was—it was—

MAURI: It was *what?*

REED: I—don't know—Mauri—

61

MAURI: *(she begins picking up her things and stuffing them into her backpack)* Yeah, well, I can tell you a couple of things *I* know, pal. I know why you're not working at that soup kitchen anymore. It's because I have a few choice documents with me about who you really are and I Xeroxed them and sent them to them. And I can tell you why Will's not returning your phone calls, too. Because I clued him in on a few things. That newspaper clipping you found is just the one I showed Will. It isn't the only one I have, you know, not by a long shot. *(She brings up a tattered manila envelope from within her backpack.)* It's all right here. Everything anyone needs to know about Reed Waters. I'll say one thing for you, though—you never went through my pack. Or if you did you never opened this envelope. I half-expected you to.

REED: What—would you have done—if I had?

> *Mauri reaches into her pocket, brings out the switchblade, quickly opens it.*

MAURI: I have this.

REED: For me? Or you?

MAURI: That's a good fucking question. I don't know. I never decided.

REED: Why—Mauri, why did you come here?

MAURI: Maybe I wanted to kill you. Maybe I wanted to kill myself, right here, with you watching. To let you know exactly what you did. What it meant.

REED: I—know—

MAURI: You don't know *shit!* *(Puts blade away, finishes packing)* What do you know? Worthless piece of garbage. Human garbage. Not *even* human.

REED: I've tried—I've tried to—to live a different kind of life—since then—

62

MAURI: A *different kind* of life?

REED: Yes.

MAURI: And what kind of life does Aunt Evie get to lead? Huh? What kind? She's dead, isn't she?

REED: Yes—yes.

MAURI: And she's gonna go on being dead.

REED: Yes.

MAURI: And you can live any *kind* of life you want to lead. You can laugh all you want and party all you want and fuck all you want and Evie will still be dead. Isn't that right, Reed? *(Zips up bag)*

REED: Yes. I'm—I'm so—

MAURI: *Don't fucking say you're sorry!*

> *Reed has fallen to his knees. She stares at him for*
> *a long moment, then rushes out.*

63

Act 2

Scene One

Reed's apartment is dark. Mauri and Will are discovered at either end of the outside area. Mauri, visibly upset, is calling him from a payphone, which may or may not actually be onstage—but she should at least be holding a receiver. Will has a cell phone in his hand.

MAURI: Will?

WILL: Mauri? Is that you?

MAURI: Yeah—yeah, it's me, Will.

WILL: What do you want?

MAURI: You sound mad.

WILL: Well, you sound like you're crying.

MAURI: I'm not crying. I'm not. You're not mad at me, are you, Will?

WILL: I never said I was mad at you.

MAURI: You stopped talking to me.

WILL: Talking to you? How could I…?

MAURI: I wasn't the one who killed her, Will.

WILL: But you—to go to him, to live with him? What is that? What kind of sickness is that?

MAURI: I'm not the sick one!

WILL: You sure about that?

MAURI: Will, don't. Please don't. I'm calling to say goodbye.

WILL: Where are you?

MAURI: At the bus station. I'm leaving.

WILL: What happened?

MAURI: He—he found out. I had to go.

WILL: Are you all right?

MAURI: Yeah…yeah.

WILL: Is *he* all right?

MAURI: *(smirks)* He's peachy-keen.

WILL: Where are you heading?

MAURI: I—I don't know. Somewhere. I—don't know.

WILL: Back home? To California?

MAURI: Oh, *fuck* no, Will. Not there.

WILL: Where, then?

MAURI: Wherever the bus takes me, I guess. I've got some money… *(She digs in her pocket, glances at the bills as she speaks)* It ought to take me somewhere. Maybe I'll go south for the winter. You know. Hang out in Florida with all the retirees. Play on the beach. Might be fun.

WILL: You don't sound like you're having fun.

MAURI: Well, I'm *going* to. When I get down there.

WILL: Mauri—what do you want to leave the city for?

MAURI: Huh?

WILL: I mean—you don't have to leave the city. Come over here, to my place. I mean, my mom's place. We can put you up for a while, until you figure out what to do.

MAURI: With all those brothers and sisters of yours?

WILL: It'd be all right.

MAURI: No thanks, Will. That's sweet of you. Really. But…no.

WILL: Don't let *him* run you out of town, Mauri.

MAURI: I'm not running out. I'm not. I just…

WILL: I wish you wouldn't just leave. Like this.

MAURI: Well, you weren't talking to me anyway, Will. I haven't heard from you since…

WILL: Come on. What did you expect? You knew what you were doing when you told me about you and your aunt and him and all that. Wasn't I supposed to have any reaction to it?

MAURI: Yeah…?

WILL: *And* to the idea of you living there? Do you think that's normal?

MAURI: Goddamn it, Will, this isn't about *me*…

WILL: I think it is. You just don't know. I think it's *all* about you.

MAURI: Fuck you.

MAURI: He did what he did. It was a long time ago. It's over. What are *you* doing?

MAURI: That's not the point.

67

WILL: That *is* the point. It's not *your* point.

MAURI: That just shows what you know, Will. That you could think it was over. That it could ever be over.

WILL: Look, Mauri, just...just stick around, okay? Come on. You can come here. I'm serious. Just get on the Metro. You know which station. I'll meet you there.

MAURI: I can't, Will.

WILL: Mauri—

MAURI: I *can't*.

WILL: So this is how it ends?

MAURI: This is how it ends.

WILL: I just—thought we had something, you know? You telling me it didn't matter?

MAURI: It didn't. It *doesn't*. Nothing matters.

WILL: And I don't think you're being fair to him, either.

MAURI: *Fair?*

WILL: He took you in, didn't he? Fed you? Gave you a place to stay?

MAURI: Did you say I'm not being *fair* to *him?*

WILL: You can't just skip how he's treated you. You can't just think about things that happened ten years ago.

MAURI: Oh, fuck off. Just fuck *off.*

WILL: You have a relationship with him now. It's not just about the past—

MAURI: I don't have any relationship with *him!*

WILL: He's treated you good, that's all I'm saying.

MAURI: And how about my aunt Evie? The person I was closest to in the world? How did he treat her? Do you want to visit her grave with me, Will? You can tell her what a great guy he is. You can lean down and talk to the fucking *dirt* and tell my aunt's rotting *corpse* what a great guy Reed Waters is!

WILL: Mauri—

MAURI: I'm going. Later, Will. *(Hangs up firmly; but then stands there for a long time, uncertainly.)*

Scene Two

*Reed is nervously tidying his apartment, clearly
expecting someone to visit. In a moment, Will
appears outside and knocks on the door. Reed
opens it.*

REED: Will.

WILL: Reed.

Pause.

REED: Come in, come in. *(Will does.)* It's—it's good to see you. Something
to drink?

WILL: I'm good, thanks.

REED: Sure?

WILL: Yeah.

REED: Well, I—sit down, Will, please. I—was happy to hear from you,
Will. I'd wondered—I thought— *(They sit. Pause.)* How are you?

WILL: I'm all right. Oh—before I forget. *(Brings out CD, hands it to Reed)*
Thanks.

REED: Of course. Will, did you get your thesis in? On Richard Wright?

WILL: Yeah. Weeks ago. Got it back, too. A-minus.

REED: Well, that's excellent. That's terrific.

WILL: Thanks for the help.

REED: Yes, sure. I— *(Another silence.)* I haven't seen you in a while, Will.
Over a month.

70

WILL: No.

REED: I was surprised when I got your e-mail. I thought…

WILL: What did you think?

REED: I—I don't know.

WILL: Mauri had a talk with me.

REED: Yes, I…she told me she had.

WILL: When did she tell you?

REED: When she left. A month ago, something like that.

WILL: Heard from her?

REED: Not a word since she left here. Haven't had any contact at all.

WILL: She called me from a bus station. Just before she left town. That same night, I think. The night she left here.

REED: Did she say where she was going?

WILL: Just that she was leaving town. That was it.

Mauri is discovered in outside area.

MAURI: Hey mister, have you got the time? Thanks. Where am I, anyway? I've been in so many places lately that they're all sort of confused in my mind, you know? I don't like to stay long in a place, know what I mean? Hey, don't go…you look like a nice guy. *(Brings her bottle from backpack)* You want a drink of this? It's good for what ails you, let me tell you. *(She drinks, offers bottle to the unseen man.)* Hey, you want to, you know, hang out? For a while? We could go someplace, you know, if you can think of someplace we could go. I'm sure we could find something to do. *(Holding her hand next to her mouth, she stretches to whisper something in his ear, then giggles.)* Yeah. You know what I mean. Hm? Sure. Let's go…

71

She exits into the darkness.

REED: So she…told you.

WILL: She told me.

(Pause.)

REED: Will, it was such a long time ago that…I—I hope that—that it… *(He gives up, defeated.)*

WILL: I thought I should hear it from you.

REED: Me?

WILL: What happened. Seemed like I—like it wasn't fair that I just stopped talking to you.

REED: Will…

WILL: But it's kind of tough, you know, learning that somebody…

REED: Will, don't…

WILL: I mean, I've known people who're in jail now. That's not hard, living where I do. I know kids who shot other kids. Went to prison when they were sixteen, seventeen. Nothin' unusual about that. My *father* got shot.

REED: I know.

WILL: But you weren't part of that. That kind of shit. When I met you it was like, here's a guy from a different world. Books. Music. "Theatah." Kind of world I wanted to be part of, you know? It seemed like you…I don't know. You cared about the kinds of things I cared about. I never met anybody like that. I never met anybody who knew the difference between Beethoven and Tchaikovksy. Shit, most of the people I knew probably never heard of either one. That's how I grew up. Two-headed calf.

72

WILL (cont'd): I wasn't into what the other kids were into. I was always off reading my books or listening to my music—which wasn't their music. I liked different kinds of things, different movies, different…everything. I wasn't like them. I knew I wasn't. They knew it, too.

REED: Yes.

WILL: I just…I've got to get *away* from there, you know? *(He jumps up, moves about restlessly.)* And it seemed like, when I met you, that…but then, when Mauri told me what she did, and showed me the things out of those old newspapers, I…I thought, Shit. He's no different. Hell, he's *worse*. Kids shooting each other up over drugs is one thing. What you did…

REED: I know.

WILL: So I…I didn't know what to do, for a while. I didn't know how to talk to you. But then I said to myself, no, I've got to give him a chance. Let him explain it. I can't just cut him off because of some old newspapers and what this girl said about him. But that, too—her being here. I just thought she was some lost kid, some girl who'd gotten herself into some trouble, but, you know, nice, really. Then she told me that…you know, who she was, how…well, that's—that's just sickness, man. Nothing but sickness. Obsession. The whole thing was too damn weird for me.

REED: I understand, Will.

WILL: *(sitting again)* So…

REED: Will…

WILL: You don't have to talk. Your business is your business, man. It's all good.

REED: It—it's not easy, Will. I've never told anyone. Psychiatrists. But not…anyone else.

WILL: Didn't you and Mauri talk about it?

REED: No. She—she just ran out. We didn't talk about it. I…I'm not sure what to say.

Mauri is discovered in outside area.

MAURI: Hey, can you guys tell me where I can score some shit? No, nothing too heavy, I just need something to clean out my head…Yeah, that'd be good. You got some? How much? Okay. *(Mimes handing money over, receiving something in return, putting it in her pocket.)* Hey, where do the kids around here go for, you know, like hookups? I need some cash. I don't think I've eaten today…Where? Oh, that corner. Yeah, I see. There aren't any, like, real hookers there, are there? They always cause trouble. Okay, great. Thanks.

She exits into the darkness.

REED: I…I don't know how to talk about it, Will. I don't know how to start.

WILL: It's okay, man. I understand. *(Stands)* It's your life, Reed. It's none of my business. I'll head out.

REED: *(stands)* No—no, Will, I don't want you to go. Please don't. It's just that…finding words is…

WILL: Yeah.

REED: Hard.

WILL: Yeah.

REED: She…Her name was Evie. Evie Singer.

WILL: She was Mauri's aunt?

REED: Yes. She…I…I knew her, I—I'd known her from before, I…I met her when…uh…*(Roaming restlessly)* Will, it was such a—a long time ago, I hardly remember…I'm trying, trying to remember…But you see, they—afterward—they put me in a, well, an institution.

74

REED (cont'd): Not a prison. A—a hospital. What happened there, it, it, it made it hard to—to remember, to think about that time in my life—so much of it just got—got burned out...

WILL: Burned out?

REED: Electroconvulsive therapy. Electroshock.

WILL: You mean where they strap electrodes onto your head and...?

REED: Yes. And drugs. They had me on a lot—a lot of drugs. Anti-depressant. Anti-psychotic. Anti-seizure. I hardly knew where I was. I hardly remember any of it. That's why—I'm trying, Will, I really am, but I just...

Mauri is discovered in outside area.

MAURI: *(bottle in hand; drinking)* Hey mister, you looking for a date? We could, you know, hang out for a while. C'mon. You know a place we could go...? What? 'Cuz I need the *money*, asshole, what do you think?...Well, *fuck you, too! (She watches him go; under her breath)* Motherfucker.

She exits into the darkness.

REED: It was—it was on a beach, and—I—she was there, we were together, I knew her—I'd known her from before—I told you that—and...the sun was—shining—there was...wind...

WILL: Reed...

REED: She was...lying there...

WILL: Reed...

REED: She was...I couldn't have...it couldn't be *me*...

WILL: Reed...

75

REED: I have nightmares about it. I can't—remember it, exactly, but I have nightmares about it. I'm on that beach, and there's the smell of the sea, that salty odor, and there's a breeze in my face—the sun is hot overhead—these black, black clouds are heading toward me over the horizon…I look down…her arm is at a strange angle, up and to the side, you wouldn't think it could have stopped…stopped just like that, but it did, and the bangles on her wrists, and…her hair…she had such long, long hair…it blew over her face…And then the sky grows dark, darker than night, and yet I can see—see everything…I hear crying—not…not hers…I knew—later, I knew…about her family. Her sister, Dorothy, she—she attended the trial, every day of it, I think…I remember seeing her there, again and again, her eyes studying me…She—she fought against my release, you know. Sent petitions to the court. I—I knew that she—that Dorothy had a daughter, but I never saw her. She must have been very small then…very—small…

Mauri is discovered in outside area.

MAURI: Fifty bucks for what…? No, I don't usually do that…'Cuz number one it *hurts,* and number two you'll probably give me fucking AIDS or something…Yeah, I bet. Shit. Look…how about fifty bucks and another bottle of this? *(Holds up bottle)* There's a liquor store right over there…Deal? Yeah, sure. Whatever you want to do. We'll use the alley over there. I don't give a fuck, really. You got the money? C'mon…

She exits into the darkness.

WILL: Reed, maybe we should just skip it. It's none of my business, I guess.

REED: To be that small, how…? I wouldn't think she would even remember…

WILL: She told me she was close to her aunt. That she was like a mother to her when she was little.

REED: Yes, yes…I never knew about that…It's astounding to think of, you know…move one grain of sand on the beach and the rest of the world is changed—changed forever…*Your* world was changed forever, Will, when—your father…

76

WILL: Yeah.

REED: People, we…we don't know what we're doing…we have no idea of the enormity of things.

WILL: Yeah.

REED: We just have to—to live, somehow, to go on—living…

Mauri is discovered in outside area.

MAURI: *(Staggering)* Steven? Steven, Steven, where are you, Steven? I'm sorry. I told you I was sorry. What else am I supposed to say? Steven? Where are you? Are you here, Steven? Come out where I can see you. I'm sorry, I'm sorry, I'm sorry, Steven…I told you, I'm sorry, I'm so sorry… Steven, come out…Steven…

She exits into the darkness.

REED: *(recovering; sitting)* Will, I'm sorry. I'm sorry for everything.

WILL: You don't have to say that to me.

REED: I do. I am.

WILL: It just makes it—weird.

REED: I know.

WILL: I'll have to think about it. All of it.

REED: I understand.

WILL: I mean…

REED: Yes?

WILL: You *have* helped me, you know. I haven't forgotten that. I never will.

REED: Good. That's good.

WILL: But...

REED: I know.

WILL: Can you give me time to think about it?

REED: All the time in the world, Will. All the time you need.

WILL: It's funny. I can't picture it. You. Doing what you said. What she said. I can't picture it at all.

REED: I can't picture it either. I can't believe it. There are times—I wake up from these nightmares I have and I think to myself, No, that didn't happen, it can't have happened, not to *me*. As if I'm living someone else's life. It was so long ago, and I remember so little of it, yet...

WILL: Yeah.

REED: Yet it was me. I know that.

WILL: Yeah.

REED: Even if it seems impossible. It was me. I—I moved the grain of sand, I changed—changed the future forever.

Mauri is discovered in outside area.

MAURI: *(on phone)* Mom...? Yeah, it's me...I'm—I'm not sure where I am. Honestly. I've been in a lot of places lately... Mom, I was thinking—about that guy? The guy that, you know—the guy that killed Aunt Evie...? Well, I've been thinking about it, the whole thing. Why did he do it...? I'm not being morbid. I know it was a long time ago. But Aunt Evie was *important* to me and I never really understood...What? I told you, Mom, I don't know...No, I don't think coming home for Christmas would be a good idea...I just don't...Yeah, well, James has something to do with it, yeah...Mom, I *gave* him a chance. He kept touching me and saying things to me and you *never* believed me...*I wasn't lying!*

78

MAURI (cont'd): Shit, you're the one who said I was hot for him. When I was *eleven*…Mom, you are so full of shit…That is *not* the way it was, and you know it…*That's not true!* Why do you *always* take his side! Mom, Mom…I wasn't even calling to talk about this shit…Yeah, yeah, *shit* is what it is.!…I was calling about Aunt Evie. About the guy who killed Aunt Evie. I wanted to know what you could tell me about…It does matter! It matters to me! It…*No!* Look, never mind, I'm hanging up now. Don't look for me. Yeah, I'll bet you're not. Fucking bitch. Hanging up. Hanging up. *(She does. She drops down then, burying her face in her hands.)*

WILL: *(standing to leave)* Look, Reed…I'll see you.

REED: Okay, Will. *(Stands)*

WILL: And I'll…I'll get back to you.

REED: I hope that you do.

WILL: It's just…it's just weird. For me.

REED: I know it is, Will.

WILL: I need time.

REED: I know you do.

WILL: *(at door)* But I…I wish you well, Reed. I wish you well.

REED: You too, Will.

> *They look at each other. Will exits. Reed drops down to chair, face in his hands.*

Scene Three

Darkness.

Offstage, Reed cries out. Lights come up dimly, suggesting night. Outside, Mauri approaches the door hesitantly. She has visibly deteriorated: dirty, rings under her eyes. She drags her backpack behind her. She knocks softly, much too softly to be heard. Stands waiting, looking around. Knocks softly again.

Reed appears, just awakened, running his hand through his hair. He turns on a lamp or two, then goes to the kitchen. He has not heard the knocking.

Mauri presses her ear to the door, listening.

MAURI: *(whispering)* Reed? *(Softly knocks again)*

REED: *(reacting)* Is someone there?

Mauri knocks softly again.

REED: Is someone at the door?

MAURI: *(whispering)* Reed....

Reed goes to door, listens.

REED: Will, is that you?

MAURI: *(whispering)* Reed....

REED: *(listening)* Is someone at the door?

MAURI: *(the whispering and knocking slightly louder now)* Reed...

80

*Reed realizes who is there. He backs away from
the door. Stands indecisively.*

REED: Mauri?

MAURI: It's…it's me, Reed…

REED: What—what are you doing here?

MAURI: You can tell me to go to hell if you want. I'll understand.

REED: What are you doing here?

MAURI: I was—wondering…

REED: Yes?

MAURI: I—I haven't eaten in a couple of days. I thought—you don't have to let me in…But if you could let me have, like, some bread or something…I could back away…you could just throw it on the porch…I wouldn't—wouldn't mind…Just…I'm sorta hungry…

*Reed opens door. They look at each other
tentatively.*

MAURI: Hi.

Long pause.

REED: Come—come in.

MAURI: *(hesitating)* Sure?

REED: Yes, of course. Come in. *(She does.)* What—would you like?

MAURI: Anything.

REED: There's fruit there. On the counter.

81

MAURI: Thanks. *(She goes to the fruit bowl, begins eating.)*

REED: *(sitting)* I didn't know you were in town.

MAURI: Got here an hour or two ago. On the bus.

REED: You've been gone a while.

MAURI: I don't even know—how long. Kinda lost track.

REED: Well, you left here—almost two months ago.

MAURI: Really?

REED: It was fall when you came. Winter now.

MAURI: It's cold outside, I know that. *(Pause; she eats.)* I didn't think you'd let me in.

REED: Well—

MAURI: I wouldn't have. If I was you.

REED: I've wondered where you were.

MAURI: Oh yeah?

REED: Yes.

MAURI: Well, I—I've been a lot of places.

REED: Are you all right, Mauri?

MAURI: No. I'm not all right. I'm... crazy. I think I'm— I'm going crazy. I see weird things... I hear weird things...

REED: You don't look well.

82

MAURI: I'm not well. The food helps, though. Seems like you're always feeding me…

REED: Well—I always have lots of food.

MAURI: You didn't have to let me in. You could have thrown it on the porch.

REED: It's all right.

MAURI: How—how have you been?

REED: Me? I'm all right, I guess. I saw Will a couple of weeks ago.

MAURI: Oh, yeah?

REED: He came by. We had a talk.

MAURI: How was it?

REED: I—I don't know.

MAURI: Reed, I'm—I'm sorry I did that.

REED: You don't have to say that.

MAURI: I do too. Not that it does any good. 'Sorry' never did anybody any good in the history of the world.

REED: That might be true. I don't know.

MAURI: And about your job. I'm sorry about both of them.

REED: There's nothing to be sorry about.

MAURI: Yes, there is.

REED: You just told everyone the truth. That's all you did. I was the one who was lying.

MAURI: You never lied.

REED: Deliberately misleading people is the same as lying, Mauri. No, you—it's all right. Maybe it's for the best, I don't know. I just wish you didn't hate me. But there's nothing I can do about that.

MAURI: I don't hate you, Reed. *(Leaves counter area, drops onto sofa.)* I used to. I don't anymore. It's a lot harder to hate someone when you— know them. *(Sighs)* Anyway, I don't think I can hate anybody anymore. I haven't got the energy to hate people.

REED: Are you sick, Mauri?

MAURI: Probably. I—probably. The world's weird now.

REED: I'll light the fire. How about that? You know I always keep one of those instant logs in here.

He stands, lights the "fire."

MAURI: I just feel so tired.

REED: You can rest there. It's all right.

MAURI: Thanks. I'll leave soon, though.

REED: Well, that's up to you.

MAURI: Jesus, this is like my first night here. Remember?

REED: I remember.

MAURI: I was feeling like shit. You fed me and made a fire.

REED: I remember.

MAURI: Only everything's different now.

REED: Yes.

84

MAURI: I screwed everything up.

REED: You took your shoes off, that first night.

MAURI: I guess I did. *(Begins removing shoes and socks. Reed returns to his chair.)*

REED: Mauri, why did you come here?

MAURI: *(stopping)* I didn't have any other place to go.

REED: Your parents…?

MAURI: Oh, shit. *(Resumes taking off shoes and socks.)* No improvement there.

REED: Have you talked to them?

MAURI: I talked to *her.* It was the same thing as before. She accused me of being a liar, of trying to steal her husband, blah blah blah. No, that's—over.

REED: You're fifteen years old, Mauri.

MAURI: Yeah. I know. *(Stretches feet toward fire.)* This is good. Really good. Just like before.

REED: What I mean is, you may end up in a foster home or something. If…

MAURI: They have to find me first. And they're not even looking.

REED: Mauri, I'm sure they are.

MAURI: I asked her. They're not.

REED: Well, the police…

MAURI: Reed, there are thousands of kids out there. Everywhere. Every city. I've met them. Nobody knows who they are. Nobody gives a shit. They just blend into the scenery. They steal stuff to eat. Live out of dumpsters. Guys come to fuck them and give them money to live on. Eventually the kids grow up and get jobs…or they don't grow up. I figure I can stay under the radar for a while. If I can make it 'til I'm eighteen, then I'm done. I can go out and live like a normal person. If there really are normal people.

REED: Three years of living like this?

MAURI: I'm almost sixteen. It's more like two.

REED: Still…

MAURI: I've heard there are ways of getting emancipated from your parents, but I can't go into all that shit. It's too much trouble. I'd have to go back to L.A., I'd need a lawyer, court…I can't do that. I'll just live and let live. Only…*(head in hands)* I wish…

REED: What?

MAURI: Nothing. I don't know. I don't wish anything in particular, I guess. I just wish.

REED: Mauri—

MAURI: It's just that I can't really *see* the future, you know? I can't…I can't see past today. Past right now. Everything past this is just—darkness.

REED: Maybe you should clean up, Mauri. Take a shower. That'll help.

MAURI: Maybe it would.

REED: I can put your clothes in the machine. Clean them up, too.

MAURI: Okay. I don't care. I hate to leave the fire, though.

REED: A hot shower will do wonders for you. And then you can come back to the fire.

86

MAURI: Okay.

> *She takes her backpack, gives him dirty clothes,*
> *then heads off to bathroom. Reed looks through*
> *the grubby things, then stands and cleans up the*
> *counter area where Mauri had been eating. He*
> *goes back to sofa, gathers her dirty things, moves*
> *back in direction of bathroom. Mauri appears,*
> *partly undressed, with a large bottle of aspirin*
> *in her hand.*

MAURI: Reed, I have an idea.

REED: Yes?

MAURI: Let's die together.

REED: What?

MAURI: You and me. Let's die together.

REED: Mauri, what—?

MAURI: You've got way more than enough here. I know how to do it. We should get some juice. And then some food, like bread or yogurt or something like that. If you take them on an empty stomach you'll throw them all up.

REED: Mauri, what are you talking about?

MAURI: You and me. Do you want to?

REED: I—no. No, Mauri, I don't want to. Commit suicide? No. *(He goes to her.)* Look—give me the bottle, okay?

MAURI: Why not? Do it, I mean.

REED: I—I don't want to, Mauri. I want to go on living. I can't explain it. Just—

87

MAURI: Then I'll do it. Myself.

REED: Mauri, no.

MAURI: I'll leave. I'll take the pills with me and go somewhere.

REED: Mauri—

> *Mauri approaches sofa, drops down into it,*
> *bottle in hand. She pours out the pills and plays*
> *with them throughout this speech. Reed watches*
> *her closely.*

MAURI: You know they've got a nickname? The kids I was telling you about? In some cities, anyway. They call them the Auschwitz kids. You know, like the concentration camp? They're the kids in any city who are just completely fucked-up, totaled. Been on the streets too long. Starving too long. They get weird diseases and shit. Half of them have AIDS. Their families kicked them out of the house and never looked for them. Or they were abused at home, their dads were fucking them or something, and they ran away. They live in abandoned warehouses and places like that. You don't see them in the day. They're like vampires. At night they come out, all skinny and pale, half of them shaking like they've got palsy, and they hit street corners in the shitty parts of town where guys in cars pick them up and fuck them for five or ten bucks. They're, like, at the bottom. They're not even on the level of the runaways who get pimps who take most of their money but who at least protect them, sort of. That's, like, a different thing. Those kids have got kind of like a social structure or something. But the Auschwitz kids are the ones who've dropped down even farther than that. They've gotten too sick or they're too fucked-up in the head. Nobody cares about them at all. Nobody. They dumpster-dive for old hamburgers and shit and sell their asses to guys who fuck them and then leave them laying there in some alley like roadkill. They wind up dead all the time. They disappear. Their bodies are found in those same dumpsters. Naked, bruised, torn up. Dead. Girls, especially. Nobody cares. They're like cats that nobody really wanted that ran away from home one day and got run over. Somebody just scoops up the carcasses and throws them away. Nobody cares.

REED: *(close to her)* Mauri—

MAURI: That's what's gonna happen to me. I know it. That's where I'm headed. I still get good money—you know some guys pay fifty bucks to do shit to me?—but it's all downhill. It happens to all of them. They start to get that look after a while, a weird gleam in their eyes. They're strung out on drugs, they're sick…I haven't got that look yet, I don't think. But I will.

> *Reed carefully takes the bottle from her hands and begins gathering the pills and putting them back in. She does not resist. She touches and nuzzles him like a sleepy child.*

REED: I care about you, Mauri.

MAURI: I know you do. That's the weird part.

REED: Why is it weird?

MAURI: You know.

REED: What I mean is…you're not an Auschwitz kid. I care about you. Will cares about you.

MAURI: I don't think Will cares about me anymore.

REED: He asked about you. When he was here. He wanted to know if I'd heard from you.

MAURI: Oh, yeah?

REED: Mauri…I won't tell you that your parents care about you. I think they must, but maybe they don't. Maybe you're right about that. I don't know. But I care about you. And I don't want you to hurt yourself.

MAURI: *(touching bottle weakly; no real resistance)* It wouldn't hurt. I've read all about how to do it. I went into a library and used one of their computers to look it up online. You take them slowly, one at a time, with something like yogurt, peanut butter…

REED: *(closing up bottle)* Mauri...I think maybe I should—call someone.

MAURI: *(suspicious)* Who?

REED: Just...someone. A hospital.

MAURI: Why?

REED: I think you need help. I think—

MAURI: I don't need any help.

REED: You do—

MAURI: This is between you and me, Reed. Nobody else.

REED: What is?

MAURI: This. The whole thing. *(Moves away from him)* Don't call any hospitals.

REED: Mauri...

MAURI: If you call anybody, I'll have quite a story to tell them. Ever thought of that, Reed? *(Stands, moves restlessly)* I can tell them all about the weird middle-aged murderer from the crazy house who took me in and then *raped* me every night.

REED: That's not true—you know it's not true.

MAURI: They'll believe it. Anybody would. Nobody would believe you're so goddamn *good*. They'll lock you up so fast you won't even know what happened.

REED: Mauri—

MAURI: Just—*don't call anybody,* okay?

REED: Okay.

MAURI: Aw, shit! *(Sudden wave of emotion; she drops back down to sofa)* Reed...I need to know something.

REED: What?

MAURI: You know what.

REED: Mauri—I can't—

MAURI: Maybe—if I could understand—

REED: I—hardly remember...

MAURI: You must remember it. You can't not remember it.

REED: Only some...They burned out the rest.

MAURI: Please, Reed. We're *connected,* don't you see? I have to—have to understand...

REED: They put electrodes on my head and burned out the rest.

MAURI: Just tell me what you remember. Please.

REED: What good...?

MAURI: I don't know. But I need it. I need to...I guess that's why I came in the first place, Reed. To know.

REED: It was so long ago...

MAURI: Not to me it wasn't.

> *Pause. Reed moves to the kitchen, puts the bottle on a high shelf, returns to her.*

REED: Won't it just hurt you? To hear it?

MAURI: I can't be hurt by it any more than I already have been.

*They study each other. Long pause. Throughout
the following section, as Reed struggles to tell the
story, Mauri's interpolations are uniformly gentle
and supportive.*

REED: Will asked me—the same thing…I couldn't say much…I tried.

MAURI: Try with me.

REED: It's a long story.

MAURI: I've got nothing but time, Reed.

REED: Well—will you tell *me?*

MAURI: Tell you what?

REED: Your secrets. What you were doing during all that time after you discovered where I was but before you showed up here. Who Steven is.

MAURI: What did you say?

REED: Steven. Who he is.

MAURI: How do you know that name?

REED: Will you tell me, Mauri? It's the only way.

MAURI: Okay. You first, though.

REED: Do you promise you'll tell me? After I finish? You'll tell me everything?

After a long time, she slowly nods.

MAURI: I can take it if you can.

REED: I…All right. You…I guess you know what happened to your aunt.

92

MAURI: You strangled her.

REED: Yes. In the dunes of the beach near where we—we both lived—on the California coast…but that was later. I'd met her years before. Ten years before. When she was…

MAURI: Go ahead.

REED: I can't.

MAURI: You can. I know you can.

REED: I lived in a room over a garage that my father owned, right at the beach, in this town called Satin. I was nineteen—this was twenty years ago.

MAURI: Okay.

REED: I'd had—problems. Probably ever since my mother died. My father and I hardly spoke. I didn't have any friends. I was alone all the time. I had a job, but—I was alone all the time. Too much of the time. Well, I was walking on the beach one morning—it was a hot, clear day, but the beach was deserted because there was a parade downtown. A—girl…your aunt…I mean, she would become your aunt, later…she was walking all by herself toward me. She had on a white bikini and a big floppy sun hat. Her hair was long, dark, flowing out from under the hat. Barefoot. Just all by herself. She was…beautiful. I'd never seen anyone so beautiful. Well, we… we were the only two people on the beach, and we said hello. I—I bought her an ice cream cone. We…Mauri, this part is—awkward…

MAURI: Tell me.

REED: She was…a sweet girl, beautiful…she was very young, fifteen— my God, that's your age now, isn't it? But I was only nineteen…She told me she was visiting with her family but that she hated parades and that she'd decided to wander the beach by herself while her parents and sister— your mother, your mother later—went to it. We talked, we…we climbed around in the dunes…

93

MAURI: Did you have sex with her?

REED: I…Yes. It was…I'd never even had a girlfriend before. I'd never been on a *date*. It was…indescribable. I fell in love with her that afternoon, her face, her voice, her body, her laugh…

MAURI: She had a great laugh.

REED: Yes. She did. She…we spent hours together, that day. And then she had to go, back to her family. She lived in northern California. We said we'd see each other. We gave each other our phone numbers…I was…I can't explain what happened to me. Mentally. I was…Well. The world had—had changed for me. That day. Completely. And…But when I called her, called the number she'd given me, it was the wrong number. But—I don't know. I didn't take the hint. I…I knew her name, Evie Singer, and I went to the library, found all the Singers in the phone book who could be her family in the town she mentioned…I called and called…Finally I got the right one. It's odd—but as I think of it now, I realize—I never thought of this before—that the person who initially picked up the phone was her sister. Your mother. When she was—I don't know, sixteen or seventeen.

MAURI: Aunt Evie was two years younger than my mom.

REED: Yes, well…I talked to her. To Evie. She said she'd done some things she was embarrassed about now and that she just wanted to forget it. She was—nice. Polite. She apologized. But she hung up. I…I went up there, a few weeks later. Found her coming home from school. She didn't even recognize me at first. Then she apologized again, said that last summer was strange for her, she wanted to move on. She…I think she was…even a little—afraid of me. Afraid that I'd come all that way, that…

MAURI: Tell me, Reed.

REED: I sent her letters. I…Eventually I got a visit from a policeman. A detective. Evie had been showing the letters to her parents. He—he made it clear I wasn't to write to her anymore. And I didn't. Not at all. Not once. But I…I did go up there a few times. I drove past her house, their—house. I saw her walking now and then.

94

MAURI: You were stalking her.

REED: I never thought of it that way. Not even when I started collecting things about her. I subscribed to her hometown paper, looked for mentions of her name. By sending them a donation I got on the mailing list of her school, using a different name, and that got me the school paper every month. I knew she was on the volleyball team, knew she was in the debating club. I even drove up and saw her in her school play. I knew when she'd been accepted to college in Los Angeles. I knew what college it was. I knew what she was majoring in. I…But that was all, you understand? I just…followed her. Like a fan follows a celebrity. I never meant any harm. As I got older it just became…a habit. She never knew. No one did. I never got in any more trouble about it. I just…watched her. From afar. You know, in that period I went to junior college for a while, and I even had a girlfriend. Wendy. A sweet girl, pretty. We got along. But it never stopped my…

MAURI: Obsession?

REED: I knew when she graduated. I knew she went back to her hometown. I knew when she got married. But…It was all right. All of it. I wanted nothing from her.

MAURI: I don't remember her husband. She wasn't married long.

REED: No, she—she wasn't. Finally—this was ten years after we'd first met, on the beach, the day we'd made love on the beach, the day…ten years later, her hometown paper announced that she was leaving the area to take a job in Satin. My God, what were the odds? She was coming to live in Satin, California? It was—unbelievable. It was terrifying. I didn't know what to do. So I…I didn't do anything. I just went to my job, came home…I lived in a little apartment then, not far from that room over the garage I'd lived in before…I saw her one day. She was the manager of a shop on the beach. I walked in, I…I was just another customer. She didn't know me. I looked different—ten years had gone by, after all. My long hair was gone. I had glasses. We talked. I bought a little money clip. She was wearing a bright flowery pants suit with big bangle earrings. Her hair was still wild, still—she was—older, but the same…remarkably the same…

MAURI: I remember when she moved away. I cried and cried. We spent so much time together—my mom was always out, always drinking…She had to promise to drive up and see me every month. I was five. But I remember it like it just happened last week.

REED: Yes. Well, I—I asked her on a date. She still didn't know me, had no recollection of me. It had been ten years. And we…*(saying it is agony for him)*…we went to the beach, the same beach, it was…it was a warm summer's day, and I…I started talking, I…we were getting along so well, I started talking as we tramped back into the dunes, reminding her how she'd been here before, and then saying all the things I knew about her that I—I shouldn't have known—she became frightened, and she remembered—remembered *me*—I—I just wanted it to be like it was, that day, that day ten years before, I…But something happened. When she tried to run I—I can't…

MAURI: Tell me, Reed.

REED: I can't remember then. All I remember is that I was kneeling over her. She was on her back, her arm was at a strange—strange angle, and… her hair…it was—it was around her neck, it was blowing across her face…I looked up…dark clouds were rushing up, the wind had whipped up…

MAURI: It's okay, Reed.

REED: They found me only an hour or two later. In my apartment. I had all the things, all her things, out…all the newspapers, all the photos, all…in my arms…I was crying…That's all I remember. That's all. *(Pause)* Later, there was a—a trial, I guess—it's all very vague in my mind…I… my father, he…my father…

MAURI: What about your father, Reed?

REED: He hired a lawyer for me. He came to the trial. I remember that. But at the end, when they took me to the—to the—

MAURI: The institution.

REED: He—he—later I found out that he'd gone home that day and started up one of his cars in the garage with the door closed and…and…

MAURI: He killed himself?

REED: And I…I *inherited his money*, do you understand? I killed him…

MAURI: You didn't kill him, Reed.

REED: I killed him. What I did killed him. He couldn't go on living. And I inherited his money. Later, when I was released, they…I inherited his money. I killed him and then I inherited his money.

Long pause.

MAURI: I wish I understood why I don't hate you.

REED: You should. Hate me.

MAURI: I used to. I can't anymore. I just—I just want to die. To *stop*. It all—hurts. It all hurts too much.

REED: Yes. It does.

MAURI: Everything just hurts. All the time.

REED: Yes.

MAURI: It hurts and it never stops hurting.

REED: Yes.

A sudden, tender touch between them.

MAURI: Does everybody live like this? With this much—hurt?

REED: I don't know.

MAURI: They can't. The *world*—it couldn't go on.

REED: But we go on. Somehow.

MAURI: How? When we've done such bad things?

REED: We?

MAURI: Bad things, terrible things, unforgivable things.

REED: Why did you say 'we,' Mauri?

MAURI: I've done bad things. Everybody's done bad things.

REED: But unforgivable?

MAURI: Unforgivable.

REED: Not many people do unforgivable things, Mauri. I did. Not many do.

MAURI: I did, too. *(Pause)* I did an unforgivable thing.

REED: Getting me fired isn't unforgivable, Mauri.

MAURI: I don't mean that. I mean something else.

REED: Steven?

MAURI: Reed, how do you know that name? You said it before.

REED: I heard you say it. When you were so sick, that first night. As you were falling asleep. And I heard it again later, when you were getting better. You mumble in your sleep, you know.

MAURI: Yeah, I—I know.

REED: Who is Steven, Mauri?

MAURI: I—I've never told anybody about Steven.

REED: You can tell me. What reason in the world would there be not to tell me—now?

> *Long pause. A clear role-reversal occurs now:*
> *Mauri becomes the tortured storyteller, Reed the*
> *calm and supportive listener.*

MAURI: Maybe you're right. Tonight, it—tonight could be the end of the world.

REED: It could be, I suppose.

MAURI: It could all stop in the next hour. God could reach down—or the nuclear bombs could land—or—I'd like that. Somebody to step in somehow, say, 'Okay, it's over now.' And everything just ends. Just like that. Maybe somebody will. I hope they will. Even right now. This minute.

REED: Who is Steven, Mauri?

MAURI: *(sighs)* I told you about Alan, right?

REED: Your boyfriend. The one you thought was your boyfriend. Yes. The—inititation.

MAURI: Yeah. Well. I didn't tell you—I didn't tell you the rest of the story.

REED: You told me you'd been gang-raped. You told me you ran away after that—ran away from home. And that you came to the hospital to find me.

MAURI: Yeah. But that—leaves some stuff out. Actually what I did was—when I left, home I mean, I didn't leave right then, like I said. I lied about that. I just—I went home, took the longest, hottest shower I've ever taken in my life. I didn't cry or anything. I just…I just went back to normal living, you know? It wasn't until…Well, that's when I started thinking more and more about Aunt Evie, about how my life changed when she died, how one person I'd never even seen changed everything about my life. Something had to happen, I had to *do* something.

99

MAURI (cont'd): I couldn't tell anybody. Least of all my fucking *mother*. Well…Shit, I missed my period. I knew what that meant right away, but I tried not to think about it. Then I missed it again and…well. I didn't know what to do. Everybody was against me. Except Evie. Evie had never been against me. But she was…

REED: Yes.

MAURI: When I was about four months, I took all the money I had, and I stole some from my mom's bedroom too. And I stopped at the bank where I had an account and took out everything. I had this weird idea that I was gonna go get a job somewhere—like anybody was gonna hire a homeless kid with no parents to do anything. I just wanted to—to get away from everything I'd ever known. I *had* to, you know? After—what happened. It was that or—die.

REED: Yes.

MAURI: I had to become a new person.

REED: Yes.

MAURI: Only it turned out I didn't. I just hauled the same old person around with me, like a goddamn—*corpse* on my back. But the corpse was—was *me*, you know?

REED: That's what happens.

MAURI: I just wandered around. I didn't do shit. Just traveled. On buses, mostly. I saw the insides of a lot of Greyhound stations. I couldn't believe how fast the money went. I had hundreds of dollars on me when I started out, but even the shittiest motel rooms cost money. Food. I didn't start turning tricks until later. Then I just—every now and then I'd ask at a restaurant or something if I could wash dishes, but…I didn't have an address, I didn't—they knew I was just a runaway who would probably steal them blind. And I would have, too. Plus the fact that I was starting to show. Pretty soon they could see I was pregnant. That didn't help.

REED: I'm sure.

100

MAURI: I just kept on, I just kept spending money. I stopped staying in rooms mostly, just tried to sleep in alleys, like some stray cat. Stole shit to eat. I was in—I was in bad shape.

REED: Yes.

MAURI: Well, finally I was in Wyoming—yeah, I ended up in bumfuck Wyoming, of all places—and I had to get a room. I *had* to. I thought I was gonna die. I used my last money to rent this dumpy room in a place called Casper. Casper, Wyoming. Just a shithole. Mold in the bathtub, toilet all black, the mirror broken. I was having pains. Labor pains. It was like I was being ripped in two. It was unbelievable. But I couldn't...couldn't call anybody, or anything. There was nobody to call. I remember it was snowing outside, snowing like hell. And I was in this shithole motel room squatting over the bathtub crying and my guts felt like they were coming out... *(becoming tearful)* And this *thing*, this *baby*, started coming out of me and there was blood and junk everywhere, like fucking World War Two, you know? And it came out and came out and the umbilical cord and...I'd decided that if it was a girl I'd name it Evie, and if it was a boy I'd name it Steven because Steven has the name Eve right in the middle of it. That's the funny thing. The whole time I was pregnant it just wasn't real to me. I never thought I would actually have a baby. It was impossible. I couldn't have a baby. I *knew* I couldn't. Yet at the same time I picked out names for it. It was like I was two different people, one who was actually going through it and denying everything and another who was looking down and knew exactly what was going on.

REED: Yes.

MAURI: So...so there it was. It came out. It was *so small*. I put it in this towel that got all bloody. I thought it couldn't be alive, it was so early, but it was kicking. And...but it wasn't *crying*, you know? It was just *kicking*. And then...And then it *stopped* kicking. It was just the tiniest thing in the world, it had the smallest little face and hands and...And I swear to God I never meant to...to hurt it, it...I ...It wasn't kicking anymore, and I thought it wasn't even alive, I thought of Alan and all those...those guys...

REED: Go on. It's all right.

101

MAURI: It was dark and I...I put my hand over its little face tight and just held it there, held it tight like one of those guys had held his hand over my face when they...and it was still, I didn't feel any pulse at all, and I...I wrapped...wrapped it up in the towel along with the, what do you call it, the afterbirth thing, the placenta, and put the towel in a bag and put some clothes on and walked out to the back of the motel where there was a dumpster and I...I threw it in. I threw...it was a boy. Steven. I threw Steven in. And then I got my things and walked out of that motel in the middle of the night and never went back there again.

Long pause.

REED: *(very gently)* And the baby died?

MAURI: Yeah. *(Long pause)* ...No.

REED: What do you mean?

MAURI: *(short of breath as she says it, eyes wide, fluttering)* No...I thought...he was dead. But when they found it...him...I saw it on TV, they were talking about it on TV, this was later, they...somebody found him just a little while after I left and...and he *wasn't* dead and they drove his little body to the hospital and...And they *saved* him, they kept him alive, only...only the guy on TV said that the exposure and the partial asph—asphyx—

REED: Asphyxiation.

MAURI: Had...had *damaged his brain* and that...that he'd be...severely... he'd have to be...life support...permanently inst...institution...*(She continues trying to talk, but is reduced to weeping, incoherent sounds)*

Pause. Reed makes a tender gesture to her. She draws back, shocked, but then accepts it.

MAURI: Why can't the world just end? Right now? Just everything go— go black. Fade out. Like in a movie. Forever.

REED: I know.

MAURI: Just stop. Everything stop.

REED: It's all right.

MAURI: Reed, let's die together.

REED: No, Mauri.

MAURI: It's easy.

REED: No.

MAURI: We're connected, don't you see?

REED: I don't want to die, Mauri.

MAURI: Like an—umbilical cord.

REED: I don't want to die.

MAURI: When I first came here—you had...different feelings about me. You—thought about me. I could tell. Don't say you didn't.

REED: Maybe I did. That was a long time ago. It's all gone now. All over.

MAURI: What, then? What'll we do? What can we do?

REED: Go on. Just go on.

MAURI: Why? I want it to end. It's dark...I'm afraid...

REED: Don't be.

Sound of rain.

MAURI: What I did—nobody can ever forgive me. Steven can't forgive me. My parents wouldn't forgive me. God won't forgive me. And you— what you did...

REED: We can forgive ourselves. We can try. It might take a long time. It might take the rest of our lives.

MAURI: I can't do it.

REED: I think you can.

MAURI: I want to die, Reed.
> *She stands. His eyes do not follow her as she moves to her backpack over the next lines.*

REED: Listen. It's raining.

MAURI: Uh-huh.

REED: Just like the first night you were here.

MAURI: Uh-huh.

REED: Remember?

MAURI: Sure. I remember.
> *Unseen by Reed, Mauri brings up the switchblade from her backpack, flips it open. She begins to move up behind him.*

REED: I thought you were just a stranger, just a—stray cat.

MAURI: Uh-huh.

REED: I had no idea…

MAURI: No.

REED: I was so—lonely…you see…

MAURI: I know.

REED: I was so happy when you came here…

MAURI: I know.

REED: I was so sad when you left.

MAURI: Yeah.

REED: I didn't—

> *From behind him, Mauri takes Reed's head gently in her hand and places the switchblade against his neck.*

MAURI: Let's die together, Reed.

REED: Is this what you want? Really what you want?

MAURI: Remember when I told you about this knife? You asked me if it was for me or for you. I said that was a good question. Well…I realize it now. It's for both of us.

REED: Is it?

MAURI: You. Then me.

REED: There will be no one left here to do it for you, Mauri.

MAURI: I'll do it myself. I'm strong enough for that.

REED: If you're strong enough for that, you're strong enough for other things.

MAURI: I'm not.

REED: I think you are.

MAURI: I'm not. I'm *not*.

REED: What would this solve?

MAURI: It would solve everything. Don't you see that?

REED: No, Mauri. I don't. I don't see that. *(He slowly begins to take the knife from her. She does not resist.)*

MAURI: Just black—blank—nothing—forever and ever.

REED: That's not a solution.

MAURI: It is to me.

REED: It's not a solution, Mauri.

MAURI: There isn't any *other!*

REED: Maybe. Maybe you're right. *(He has the blade now. He closes it, puts it in his pocket.)* Maybe there's no solution but just…to go on.

MAURI: *How?*

REED: Just by…putting one foot in front of the other. Getting to the next minute. The next hour. The next day.

> *She moves restlessly away from him.*

MAURI: And that's it? That's all it is? The whole thing? Getting to the next day?

REED: Not all. It gets better, Mauri. You can stay here. Everything's all right here. We can invite Will over. We'll all go to a concert or a movie or something. And you can go back to school.

MAURI: But it never stops hurting. That's what you said. It never stops hurting.

REED: No. It never does.

MAURI: *(sudden resolution)* I'm going, Reed. *(Pulls on whatever clothing she needs to be able to step outside)* I can't stay here. I'll go—somewhere. I'll go—I'll—

REED: *(rising)* You said that there's nowhere for you to go, Mauri.

MAURI: I'll find a place. And if I don't—if I don't—well, I can steal a big bottle of aspirin easily enough. I don't need yours. I don't suppose you'd give me back my knife?

REED: No.

MAURI: Doesn't matter. I don't need it anymore. *(Gathers backpack, heads to door)*

REED: There's nothing out there, Mauri. Nothing but the rain and the dark.

MAURI: I don't care.

REED: I can't think of you out there—lost in the rain.

MAURI: Don't worry about me. *(Opens door, rushes out. Stops after a few steps, looking around bewildered.)*

REED: *(at door)* Mauri…come inside.

MAURI: I can't.

REED: All you have to do is turn around.

MAURI: I *can't.*

REED: Come on. One foot in front of the other.

MAURI: If I go in there…everything just goes on. Nothing ends.

REED: Nothing ever ends, Mauri. Things just change.

MAURI: *(turns slowly to him)* Do they really change?

REED: They can. But sometimes they need help.

MAURI: Will you help me?

REED: If you'll help me.

> *Pause. Finally Mauri steps back into apartment.*
> *She drops her backpack, moves slowly to fire, sits*
> *down on floor before it. Reed stands behind her.*

MAURI: Remember when I told you about—about Bourne Street? Where I used to live? How I used to think of it as Mourn Street—like somebody died?

REED: Yes.

MAURI: Reed, I think I still live on that street.

REED: A lot of people live on that street, Mauri.

MAURI: Do you think we'll ever live—anywhere else?

REED: I don't know. But we can live there if we have to. We'll fix it up. We'll make it as nice as we can.

> *He kneels behind her.*

MAURI: I don't know how much longer I can live on that street. It's always—dark there. Like midnight.

REED: It won't always be dark, Mauri. The sun comes up on that street too.

MAURI: Does it?

REED: Yes.

MAURI: You promise?

REED: Yes.

MAURI: I don't know if I can wait long enough.

REED: I'll wait with you. We'll wait together.

MAURI: What if it—what if—

From behind, Reed embraces her.

REED: We'll wait right here. Until day.

MAURI: Are you sure we can make it that long, Reed?

REED: I'm sure we can try.

MAURI: And if we do?

REED: Then we'll make it to the next. And the next.

MAURI: Together?

REED: I don't know.

MAURI: Apart?

REED: I don't know.

MAURI: I'm glad I'm not out in the rain.

REED: No one should be left out in the rain, Mauri.

MAURI: I wish—oh God, I wish—

REED: What do you wish, Mauri?

MAURI: Nothing. Nothing in particular. (*Pause*) I—I just—I—I just wish...

Slow fade.

Author's Afterword:

The Road to *Mourn Street*

Publication of *Midnight on Mourn Street*, the novel, was a major event in my life in the fall of 2008. I had seen stories, poems, essays, and articles of mine appear in magazines and journals for decades—my first paid appearance in print dates back to 1986—but for a long time success as a novelist eluded me. I spent six years in the late 1980s and early '90s writing a gargantuan mainstream/literary work, *The Unspoken,* which I thought would catapult me to the top ranks of American writers immediately upon its publication; but despite the efforts of two literary agents and the opinions of several publishers who offered the manuscript glowing reviews even as they rejected it, it was never published.

So I had to go back to the drawing board. In the mid-1990s I completed—in a matter of a few white-hot months—a much shorter and more conventional novel, written in a fairly highflown literary style but structured like a straightforward psychological thriller. I gave this manuscript the stark and (I see now) unattractive title *Wreckage.* It was a third the length of *The Unspoken.* It had complex, tormented main characters with superdramatic conflicts and, I believed, a fair amount of suspense. A respected literary agent who read *Wreckage* in 1996 snapped it up, assuring me that it would be "a relatively easy sale." Two dozen publishers later, the agent returned the unsold manuscript to me.

At that point the whole idea of writing novels filled me with nothing but despair. I made no conscious choice about the matter, but most of the next decade saw no further novelistic efforts from me. I focused on other forms of writing. Books of my poems were published. An article of mine, "Southern California Sorcerers," enjoyed considerable success beginning in 1999, when it appeared in *Filmfax* magazine; it later became the introduction for a popular fantasy/horror anthology, *California Sorcery,* and has since been reprinted in a number of venues. This piece, along with several short stories which appeared in genre markets around this time, brought me a small degree of attention in the field of dark fiction—enough that I was eventually able to convince a small-press publisher to bring out a slim collection of my tales, *Thundershowers at Dusk: Gothic Stories,* in 2006.

For the first time I found myself with something resembling an audience for my fiction—a tiny one, to be sure, but an audience nonetheless. Though I am in no way a commercial writer (ask any of the agents who have ever represented my work), it certainly seemed worth considering following up the *Thundershowers* book with more in the "dark" vein with which I was enjoying some small recognition. In fact, the necessary next step was obvious. I needed a novel.

The problem was, I didn't have one. And I had no interest in trying to knock out some pulp nonsense about monsters or serial killers in order to try to make a fast buck; I doubted I could succeed at that type of game anyway. Still—once a writer has had success with short stories in a given field, the place to go is into novel-length work. But *The Unspoken* was an entirely literary effort, with no genre elements whatsoever. It was not a possibility. How, then?

In the preceding eight or nine years I'd given almost no thought at all to *Wreckage,* my failed follow-up to the failed *Unspoken.* In fact, I'd all but forgotten I'd ever written it. Several copies of the manuscript were in a dusty box in my basement, a box I'd not opened in years. But as I pondered the problem of writing a novel, my mind cast itself back to that sophomore (not to say sophomoric) effort. Most of the details of the story were lost to my memory, but I remembered enough to know that it had a kind of thriller structure. I certainly recalled the basic issues of my co-protagonists, which featured no shortage of violence and murder. *Wreckage* hadn't found a home before; might there be a possibility of resurrecting it now?

In the spring of 2006 I brought a copy of the manuscript out of its cardboard crypt downstairs and read it straight through, an experience which proved both encouraging and dispiriting. The novel had strong thematic elements, without doubt. The characters were vividly rendered. There was a good deal of enticing mystery in the early sections which resolved, I felt, quite satisfactorily by the end. All that was positive—I felt that *Wreckage* had many of the elements needed for a successful novel. But I was equally disappointed with much of it. The novel was badly overwritten; I had made the unfortunate decision to write it in the same highly erudite, literary style of my first novel, which was a poor match for this later work's more garish and sensational plot elements. Some of the writing was repetitive. And the thing was without doubt too long, with too many essentially irrelevant flashbacks and side issues. It wasn't bad, really, on the whole; but with the benefit of nearly ten years away from the manuscript, I knew I could make it much better. What's more, because of the novel's very dark themes, I felt that this, finally, could become the piece which would break me through that ultimate and most important barrier, turning me at last into a published novelist.

Well, that is the way it worked out.

In the summer of 2006 I placed the manuscript of *Wreckage* on the paper stand next to my computer (no electronic file of the original novel still existed) and began, word by word, paragraph by paragraph, page by page, to completely rewrite it. What emerged was not a *different* novel—it was the same story, with the same characters and events in mostly the same order—but a vastly better version of the *same* novel. It was leaner—fifteen percent shorter than the original—with simpler, tighter prose and no wanderings onto unimportant subplots. I christened the result of my two months' effort with a new, superior title, *Midnight on Mourn Street,* and with the friendly assistance of the novelist Gary A. Braunbeck, sold the final result to Earthling, the first publisher to whom it was submitted. *Mourn Street* was released in the fall of 2008 to considerable acclaim, including a Bram Stoker Award nomination. With those encouraging indications of success, my mission was accomplished—and I was finally finished with the novel.

What I didn't know was that the novel wasn't yet finished with me.

From the beginning, various friends and reviewers had said the same thing to me about the book—that it "would make a great movie." I didn't, and don't, agree: *Midnight on Mourn Street* is a story with basically only three characters, and a single location (Reed's apartment); moreover, much of the "action" of the novel takes place inside Reed and Mauri's minds, or else in the dialogue they speak to each other. To be adapted to film the book would have to be almost completely re-envisioned, and probably made unrecognizable in the process. (I would, of course, be delighted to let someone *try*—inquiries welcome.)

But even as I was revising the old *Wreckage* manuscript in 2006 it struck me that, while the basic elements of the novel were essentially uncinematic, they were powerfully theatrical. What were clearly disadvantages in terms of moviemaking—limited cast, limited locations, endless dialogue—were just as clearly the very elements that might make *Mourn Street* an effective stage drama.

But I had no theatrical experience whatsoever, outside of essaying a few roles in high school plays and scribbling a couple of short absurdist sketches in the manner of Pinter and Ionesco in my first years of college. Playwrights, especially Tennessee Williams and Arthur Miller, were a basic

113

part of my life's reading, but my own most fertile artistic grounds had always been in prose fiction and poetry; I was no dramatist. And yet it was hard to deny that *Mourn Street* seemed almost ready-made for the stage. There would be problems, surely—the huge amount of interior monologue, in particular, would pose a serious challenge. But a part of me insisted that I must try.

But I wouldn't do so without some sort of support from actual theatre artists. I hadn't the heart to work for months on a stage play that would only meet the same fate as had *The Unspoken*. If writing a stage script simply meant my sitting in a room, typing away with no end result beyond the pages winding up in a box downstairs, there would be no point.

As it happened, I did know a few members of a local professional drama group, The Quotidian Theatre, which performs in Bethesda, Maryland. Their dual specialties are Chekhov and the Southern dramatist Horton Foote, and I had been impressed by many of their productions. Ultimately I had met Jack Sbarbori and Stephanie Mumford, the two producer/directors in charge of the theatre, and they had found me useful as host for a couple of their post-performance talks offered to their audiences as a bit of a bonus on one or two nights of a play's run. I described to Jack and Stephanie what I had it in mind to do, and although they had no formal intern or writer-development programs in place at the Quotidian, they took me on as something of a special project. I was assigned one of their talented writer/directors, Audrey Cefaly, to act as my mentor as I began to develop the script. I wrote numerous drafts in the ensuing months, leading eventually to a table reading at which Jack offered the following laconic observation about my material: "More things have happened to the three people in this play than has happened to all the characters in every Horton Foote play I've ever directed!"

Finally, in May of 2009, there was public performance of the script directed by Norman Seltzer and featuring three fine actors—John Collins, Lenora Spahn, and Brandon Rice—at the Quotidian's main stage.

What did the novice playwright learn from this experience—about playwriting, and about the art of adaptation?

Certainly I discovered that playwriting is a highly architectural endeavor. By that I mean that a script has to be *built* in a way foreign to the writing of prose fiction. My novel has twenty-nine chapters and who-knows-how-many scenes—an impossible structure for the kind of realistic drama I sought to write. I decided at the beginning that I would eschew complex theatrical devices and the kind of cheap tricks often employed by novelists-turned-playwrights—having the characters address the audience directly, for instance. (It worked for Tennessee Williams in *The Glass Menagerie,* but I knew full well I was no Williams.) All the action of the novel had to be streamlined, telescoped, simplified. Actually, that was the most difficult aspect of the entire enterprise—figuring out how I could limit all the action to what turned out to be just seven scenes. I drew up charts (of a sort that would be anathema to my prose or poetry writing) indicating which characters would be on stage at a given moment and what they would talk about, focusing always on one piece of wisdom I'd been offered—that is, always to ask myself, "What does the audience need to learn in this scene that they don't already know?" And then to focus all the dialogue toward that end, no matter what else that dialogue may *appear* to be about.

It was exactly the right advice, and the only way to bring my unwieldy novel under control in theatrical terms.

Once the basic structure was in place, writing the play wasn't difficult. After all, I knew the characters and plot better than anyone on earth. The real challenge was trying to somehow maintain the integrity of those characters and that plot within the confines of a realistic length for the script. At times I felt that I was throwing away virtually the entire novel, having to constantly leave out elements which I had thought essential simply to save on running time. In truth, it's still a fairly long play.

As for the "art" of adaptation, I would say that what I learned is that adaptation is less art than craft. In adapting, a writer doesn't create out of whole cloth; instead he tries to *re*-create the essence of a given work in a completely different medium. Of course what results, no matter how hard the effort, is an essentially different work. I would never mistake the novel's Reed Waters with the one we meet in the play, however strong their outward similarities. Mauri is considerably wilder in the novel than in the script, partly due to that role's difficult casting considerations. And Will is both more extroverted in the play and funnier—he represented my only chance to lighten the painfully tragic material of *Mourn Street* with any hint of comedy.

And, as readers of the novel who have just finished the script will have noted, the two versions of the story have completely different endings. This is in part due to considerations of what can realistically be mounted on the small stage of a small theatre company, but mostly, I must admit, because the novel's original ending simply didn't feel right for this stage version. All the changes in method required by the stage, all the cutting of material vital to the novel but extraneous to the play, led me and the characters to a very different place at the end of the script than the one they'd arrived at in the book. I feel that both versions are valid within their own media. I hope that readers agree.

C.C.

www.ingramcontent.com/pod-product-compliance
Lightning Source LLC
Chambersburg PA
CBHW060112050426
42448CB00010B/1850